Glamour and the **Geek**
Communication Tips
from URL (Online) to IRL (In Real Life)

Glamour and the **Geek**
Communication Tips
from URL (Online) to IRL (In Real Life)

Mikki Williams
Dave Nelsen

MOUNTAIN ARBOR PRESS

MOUNTAIN ARBOR
PRESS
Alpharetta, GA

ISBN: 978-1-61005-838-4
Library of Congress Control Number: 2016913975

10 9 8 7 6 5 4 3 2   1 2 19 16

Printed in the United States of America

∞This paper meets the requirements of ANSI/NISO Z39.48-1992 (Permanence of Paper)

MIKKI WILLIAMS, CSP, CPAE Hall of Fame Speaker and TEDx speaker, was chosen as one of the best speakers in the country by Meetings and Convention Magazine along with Tony Robbins, Bill Gates, Rudy Giuliani, Lou Holtz, Zig Ziglar and Jay Leno.

She is an award-winning speaker for Vistage Worldwide, the world's leading executive organization, Master Chair of two Vistage peer advisory boards in Chicago, a global celebrity speaker and sought-after executive speaking coach.

Mikki is the creator of Speakers School™, the original Keynote Kamp™ and The Mikki Mouth Club™.

Mikki has spoken in every U.S. state, every Canadian province and every continent except Antarctica, where she can't wear her stilettos.

DAVE NELSEN is President of Dialog Consulting Group, a boutique consulting firm that uses proven social media, Internet and mobile technology tools to help business executives enhance conversations with their most important audiences.

Dave has more than thirty years of telecommunications experience and has been at the leading edge of the social media revolution since founding TalkShoe.com in early 2005.

He's been recognized as The Ernst & Young Entrepreneur of the Year, as Tech Council CEO of the Year, and as Vistage Speaker of the Year.

Dave is an engineer by training, with a Master's Degree in Operations Research from Stanford University.

INTRODUCTION

Google defines communication as:
1. The imparting or exchanging of information or news
2. Means of connection between people or places

It's hard to imagine any human endeavor, in business or in life, that isn't based primarily on communication.

In the beginning, humans communicated strictly face-to-face, or at most, over very short distances (within earshot).

Early cave art made it possible to communicate across time, although not across distance.

Next, humans developed numbers for recordkeeping. With the advent of written language, there was great fear about what would happen when humans could communicate across time and distance without speaking face-to-face. Does this fear perhaps sound familiar to you today? LOL!

With the printing press, written communication went mainstream. With the telegraph and telephone, the world began to shrink more rapidly. Then came radio, television, copiers, pagers, faxes and mobile phones.

And then came the online social networks like Facebook. (Interestingly, humans invented social networks hundreds or thousands of years before they went online. Think: Royal Society of London or the Knights of Columbus.)

Dave Nelsen joined Vistage Worldwide, a social network for CEOs and key executives, in 2003. Shortly after that, a Hall of Fame speaker named Mikki Williams spoke to his Vistage group in Pittsburgh, Pennsylvania. It was the beginning of an unlikely partnership between "Glamour" and "The Geek."

If you've never met either Mikki or Dave, you can still probably guess who's Glamour and who's The Geek.

As a world-class speaker, Mikki's expertise is in communicating IRL (in real life).

As an early participant in LinkedIn (member number: 98,323) and podcaster since 2005 (before iPhones), Dave's expertise is in communicating online, URL as it were. (URL stands for Uniform Resource Locator, the geeky acronym meaning webpage address, as in www.___)

Independently, Mikki and Dave have mastered their respective halves of the art of communication. Together, they can tell the whole story.

In today's world, business leaders (if not everyone) must master communication in both IRL and URL forums. In this book, Glamour and The Geek share their most important tips for communicating both in person and online. Applying them will help you become more successful, in business and in life.

1
SOCIAL MEDIA FOR BUSINESS: THE MOST IMPORTANT POINTS

After leaving TalkShoe.com in 2009 (a live podcasting service my team built), I decided to write a book about how small and medium-size businesses can most effectively use social media and social networking tools. That book is called "How Can I Capitalize on Social Media When My Kid Has to Program My DVR - A Busy Executive's Guide to New Tools No Business Can Afford to Ignore."

Thinking back about that book as I begin another, here are the three most important things you need to know about *social*:

1. It's not about you; it's got to be about them. If it's not valuable to your target audience, why would they devote their time and attention to you? Right...they won't. If you're pushing the same old marketing monologue (e.g., look at <u>our</u> products and services, check out the pictures of <u>our</u> company party), you're wasting their time...and your resources.

2. The majority of the economic value in social networking will come not from external communication (read: marketing) but instead from internal applications (e.g., Yammer, Chatter, Slack). These are tools that can improve communication among your employees. Even small gains in employee collaboration can result in major improvements in profitability. And that's to say nothing about improved recruiting results, longer

employee retention, better product management and enhanced customer service that can result from smart application of social networking tools.

3. Ken Blanchard once said, "None of us is as smart as all of us." Participating in social makes everybody smarter. For most companies, there's at least as much potential in *listening* as there is in *talking*. You can get new product ideas, learn about competitors' weaknesses, discover new sales opportunities and know what your coworkers know. *Social* accelerates organizational learning.

That's why your company needs to embrace external and internal social media and social network tools.

2
THE THREE Ws...
WALK, WEIGHT/WAIT,
WOW!

Begin your presentation with the three Ws:

WALK into position.

WEIGHT on both feet, shoulder width apart, forward on the balls of your feet.

WAIT for the attention of the audience. There should be a discernible pause before beginning.

WOW! Your amazing hook.

If you want to make an impact when you begin your presentation, never open with, "Good morning," or, "Thanks for inviting me," or, "Good to be here."

Open with a surprise, a shock or an interaction. Open with something that makes a connection, something that entertains or that leaves people wondering.

Be different. Be memorable. With a great hook, you'll have the audience on the edge of their seats, wanting to know what's coming. A great hook will give you a legitimate chance to have a lasting impact.

Some openings to consider: a story, a quote, a question, statistic, joke, someone's name, a date, location, music...

Juggle! Use magic. Use a cartoon or a video...I bet you're getting the idea.

3
SOCIAL MEDIA:
10 THINGS *NOT* TO DO

Social is not your father's marketing. When participating in social media and social networking in business, here are 10 basic rules about what *not* to do:

1. Don't get started in social media if you have significant product weaknesses or customer support issues. Social media makes good businesses more successful and bad businesses bankrupt.

2. Don't use social media to explicitly sell. Instead, educate, enlighten, inform and entertain your audience. In so doing, you'll position yourself and your company as experts.

3. Don't "set it and forget it." Lack of conversation makes you look worse than not showing up at all. Once started, sustain your participation and interaction.

4. Don't go negative. Never, never, never criticize your critics. Thank them for their input and do your best to address their issues. Even if you can't make your critics happy, you'll demonstrate to everyone else that your company is tuned in and responsive.

5. Don't mix personal and business accounts. In fact, make sure that your company owns your social media accounts. After an employee departs, you don't want to discover that your company social media accounts are controlled via the former employee's personal accounts.

6. Don't expect to control the conversation. Social media is not an advertisement, product brochure, newsletter, email blast or one-way monologue; it's a conversation. Conversations are bi-directional and can have rough edges. It's likely that your customers and prospects are already talking. Join in.

7. Don't worry about a little negativity. Studies show that a little negativity increases credibility and empathy. Paraphrasing Abraham Lincoln, "You can't please all of the people all of the time." Be responsive to the negative but know that such information can actually accelerate purchasing decisions.

8. Don't feel the need to talk about everything. I like sausage but I don't want to see it made. Be honest and use discretion. Authenticity is one thing; opening the kimono is something else.

9. Don't be a generalist. With literally hundreds of millions of blogs, videos, podcasts, tweets, etc. to choose from, every individual can tailor their content consumption to his or her exact interests. Focus on one topic and do it well.

10. Don't overwhelm your followers with too much information. Everybody is busy. Providing too much information is as bad as providing too little. Find the "Goldilocks Zone." As a side benefit, this helps you to focus on the content with the highest value.

4

THE POWER OF THREE

The power of three is a writing principle that suggests that things that come in threes are funnier, more satisfying or more effective than other numbers of things.

We remember things in three. This is because having both brevity and rhythm with the smallest amount of information creates a pattern. It's a tradition that grew out of oral storytelling, for example:

- Three Little Pigs
- Three Musketeers
- Three Blind Mice
- Three Stooges
- Snap, Crackle, Pop

Use the Power of Three in your presentations for greater impact.

5
THREE RULES FOR USING SOCIAL MEDIA

Have you ever noticed that eight of the Ten Commandments are things *not* to do? *Thou shalt not...*

Just two of the Commandments are affirmatives. In keeping with roughly that same ratio, to go with the ten "don'ts" of the earlier chapter, I offer three affirmatives for using social media in business.

1. **Social media is like a cocktail party.** What works or doesn't work in one of these venues applies equally in the other. <u>Good</u> cocktail party behaviors include: Asking questions, actively listening, engaging in conversations and building relationships. The same is true in social media. <u>Bad</u> cocktail party behaviors include: Talking all about you, introducing yourself and then completely shutting up (or down), and any form of active (or passive) selling. Again, the same is true in social media!

2. **P.I.E.,** an acronym that comes from the radio business. "P" stands for "personality." Social media is about people connecting with people, so be a real person and display some personality! Have you heard the old sales adage that *"People buy from people"?* That's what this is all about. "I" and "E" stand for "interesting" and "entertaining." That's what attracts

and holds their attention. If you're boring, they won't follow you for long. Practice P.I.E.

3. And the toughest of the three rules (this is where most business social media initiatives fail): Pay it forward. Start by creating value first for your target audience. Only if your initiative is valuable for them will they continue to follow what you do. With that attention comes the opportunity for a relationship.

If you follow these three simple rules, you're far more likely to connect with, and retain, your business target audience. And that means the potential for more business.

6
EARN THE RIGHT

Don't be too vulnerable, too disclosing, too "in their face," right off the bat.

I've coached and witnessed many individuals who, because of their personality or style, tend to overshare in the hopes of connecting with the audience. There are others who have a bottom line/get-to-the-point personality, and that can often appear confrontational when what you want to be is 'care-frontational.'

Avoid being "too" anything until you've delivered enough content and value that your audience likes you and trusts you...until you've earned the right.

7

LEARNING WITH GOOGLE

As Peter Senge once observed, "The only sustainable competitive advantage is an organization's ability to learn faster than the competition." If this is true, then you can't find a more valuable free tool than Google Alerts.

With Google Alerts, you can specify a word or phrase for Google to monitor; whenever they see it, they send you an email with a link to the source. Unlike with a Google search, once established, an alert brings you breaking news and continues to run forever, or so we thought.

Think about the value of Google alerting you to what your competitors just announced. What if your salespeople could get alerts about their customers and prospects? What if you could get alerts about your partners, your key suppliers, your employees? What if you could see each new RFP (request for proposal) in your industry as it hit the wire? Maybe your business would be able to "adapt more quickly."

Unfortunately, the last Google Alert I received was in early 2015. My first question was, "Is it just me?" so I Googled the question, "Is Google Alerts dying?" and found articles by Mashable, Computerworld, and BuzzFeed (inappropriately named when reporting news like this).

Alas, how are we to get timely reports about competitors, customers and partners now? How will we adapt most quickly?

More Googling revealed a possible replacement: www.Mention.com.

While it apparently works exactly like Google Alerts, it costs roughly $8.00 per month, per alert. Whoa! While I'm sure it's worth 100-times that amount I can't bring myself to pay for something that's been free for the last decade.

And then it hit me. The answer is (drum roll please): Google! It's just going to take a tiny bit more work.

Go to www.google.com/advanced_search. In the first field, you can place your desired phrase. But it's the ninth field that's the magic one: "Last Update." You can set that to "past 24 hours" and see what's just happened. If you prefer, try "past week" or "past month" instead. If the search gives you valuable results, bookmark it! Then you can rerun it at regular intervals (the "tiny bit more work" mentioned above).

You get the idea. Or if you don't, all of the instructions are on the right side of the page at Google.com/advanced_search.

All is right with the world again because you're learning faster than the competition.

8
USE THE FIVE SENSES

See - Besides the obvious Power-Point presentation, use some visual props; a photo of someone, a card someone gave you, a drawing from your child, a can of beans...

Hear - Use music (be sure to pay your licensing fee), a bell, a button that blurts out an expression, a horn...

Touch - Give out something they can hold; a laminated card with all your points on it, a Koosh ball, a ruler with your logo – something that furthers your points...

Taste - Check out your nearest candy counter for inspiration. Holidays are also a great inspiration. For example: buy *Pay Day* candy bars to celebrate a rockin' quarter sales or *Good & Plenty* for all the good ideas and plenty of them, or jelly beans for Spring, Valentine's hearts...

Smell - The most challenging sense, but I've mastered it by using Play-Doh in my presentations. Someone else suggested the smell of fresh copier paper, a distinct gum odor, a perfumed card...

Think outside the AV box and use these sensory props to make your points.

The best storytellers use particular gestures, sound effects, music – anything that adds to what is termed "multimodal communication."

Even if you feel that's not your style, remember, it's about the audience, not about you.

9
LINKEDIN – A TOOL FOR FINDING PEOPLE

You probably use Google many times a day to find information. What if there were a comparable tool for finding people, people who could be your employees, your customers, or your partners in business?

Actually, there is, although most people don't think of it or use it in this way. It's called LinkedIn, a network of roughly half a billion business professionals (and counting).

Salespeople: What if you could find a boatload (a technical term meaning hundreds or thousands) of CEOs, or any other specific job title, within 50 miles of you? LinkedIn makes it possible not just to find such target customers, but also to connect with them. It's an advanced people search tool and it's free.

Login to LinkedIn and look for the Search box at the top of the screen (on most pages). Click the "Advanced" button to the right of that box and you're in Advanced People Search mode. You can search for people based on any combination of the following attributes:

- Keywords
- First and/or last name
- Job title
- Current or past company (great for gaining competitive advantage through what I call "insider insights")
- School
- Location (by country or by ZIP Code radius)
- Industry

- Language
- LinkedIn Groups (joining a group expands your network)
- Relationship (especially valuable for reaching people one or two degrees of separation from you)

And these are just the free options. LinkedIn can also show you who knows whom. Use your connections to get introduced to people. But instead of using LinkedIn introduction tools, I recommend connecting IRL (in real life). Even in this crazy social networking age, pick up the phone and ask your connections (presumably people that you actually know) to orchestrate three-way coffees or lunches with the people you want to meet.

I like your chances against your competitors' salespeople, the ones who are still cold calling.

10
ANCHORS

An anchor is a word, a gesture or a movement that pulls the audience back to you.

For example, during his presentations Tim Gard, professional speaker, says, "Woo Hoo!" when he

is talking about something good that has happened to him and "Bummer," when something bad had occurred, then later trains the audience to say it with him during his speech.

Another pro, Larry Winget, has the audience respond to his Oklahoma accent with, "You betcha." Mark Victor Hansen of *Chicken Soup for the Soul* fame has audience members point a finger to their brain and mutter, "Mmmm, that's interesting."

Similarly, I have an audience respond to me in my New York style with a "Yo!"

Anchors can also be something specific to you; your look, your personality, your manner of speaking. Being known for always wearing a particular tie or lapel button with a phrase or a funky hat, something unique to you, anchors the audience back to you during or after the presentation.

11

LINKEDIN – THREE RULES FOR CONNECTING (AND OTHER ADVICE)

Here's a key concept to keep in mind when using LinkedIn: You should request and accept connections with only known and trusted business associates. When it comes to connections, LinkedIn is about quality, not quantity. Your network will degrade to useless noise the more often you connect with people that you don't know. In building connections, ask yourself these three questions:

1. Do I know this person professionally?
2. Do I respect this person professionally? (As Dr. Evil says in the Austin Powers movies, "Why must I be surrounded by idiots?")
3. Would I be happy to help this person with something if he or she asked me?

When the answer to all three questions is yes, the connection request is coming from someone you can assist in making professional connections to help sell products or services, find great partners and recruit outstanding employees.

Equally as important, that person can do the same for you. If you've made the mistake of accepting every connection request coming your way, you're what I call a promiscuous linker. I recommend some unlinking. To do so, when viewing a person's profile, you'll see a blue button labeled "Send a message." On the right edge of that button you'll see a drop-down arrow. Clicking it will reveal the option to "Remove connection."

Don't worry. The person will not be notified. Please feel free to "Ignore" connection requests from people who don't meet your criteria.

With LinkedIn, a requester will not know that you've ignored his or her request. There's no explicit notification. Although choosing connections you trust creates a powerful network, you still might not want your connections to see all of your other connections, which happens by default with LinkedIn.

If your connections represent your existing customers, your hot prospects and your best employees and partners, others could use that information to your disadvantage. To prevent this, I recommend turning off connection visibility.

To do so, hover your cursor over your miniature photo in the upper-right screen area and select "Privacy & Settings." You'll land on a screen that includes a variety of privacy controls.

Click on "Select who can see your connections" and set it to "Only you." As LinkedIn will tell you, people will still be able to see shared connections, a highly valuable aspect of LinkedIn, but this represents just a small fraction (perhaps less than 1%) of your network relative to any given searcher.

With these steps completed you'll be ready to put LinkedIn to work for your business.

12
ELEVATOR SPEECH

An elevator speech is a brief message about who you are, what your business is or a project you're pitching. It's just a couple of sentences that intrigues your listener and makes them want to know more about you.

Many people feel an elevator speech needs to let people know what you can do for them; others feel it should simply be about you and what you do.

The only rule for me is that there are no rules. I've used a variety of elevator speeches; some designed to do the above, some designed just to create a WOW moment. The important thing is to have a goal as to what and why it is.

Some of my elevator speeches include, "I help people survive boring presentations." That one usually garners a laugh and peaks interest. I've also used, "I'm in the emotional transportation business."

The goal is that they always ask me what that means and that it starts a conversation.

So...imagine you're in an elevator with someone you want to impress. You have 30-60 seconds in this quick elevator ride to get them interested.

That's your elevator speech.

13
LINKEDIN – A TOOL FOR COMPETITIVE ANALYSIS

In 2005, I started a live podcasting service called TalkShoe.com. Since then more than 1,000,000 podcast episodes have been recorded using the service. But I nearly abandoned the idea less than one month after starting the company.

Here's the story of how TalkShoe came to be, and the single best trick I've ever learned in business (it involves social networking).

TalkShoe's first employee was Aaron Brauser. His job as a product manager was to define the features of the initial product by doing market research and competitive analysis. Shortly after getting started, Aaron reported that he'd found another company doing the exact same thing. They'd been around for five years, they'd raised an estimated $50 million and almost no one had ever heard of "Ingenio."

If $50 million can't put a company on the radar screen there must be a fatal flaw in the business.

My first thought was to calculate the cost of two weeks' severance pay for Aaron. I have ideas all the time and if this was a loser, let's move on (easy for me to say).

But I had a second thought. Fifteen months earlier I had joined a little business networking service called LinkedIn as member number 98,323. What if I could find and talk to some former employees of Ingenio? I might learn what they did right and wrong and benefit from their five years of experience in what I was planning to do.

Did you know that LinkedIn can show you a list of people who used to work for any company (i.e., your competitors)? These are people who have incredibly valuable experience, contacts and "insider insights." And there are a lot of these people. Most companies have two to four times as many former employees as current employees listed in LinkedIn.

In 2005 LinkedIn was small, my number of connections was small and Ingenio was small. Still, an Advanced People Search revealed nine former employees of the company. Looking at their past job titles I selected a former VP of Business Development and reached out through a mutual connection.

Long story short: A one-hour conversation with this former executive gave me two key insights into how to succeed where Ingenio had failed.

Aaron and I moved forward with TalkShoe and did indeed succeed.

Next time you're looking for insider insights (respecting others' intellectual property of course) try this Advanced People Search trick. It's the most valuable technique I've ever discovered for finding competitive information to help you be more successful in your business.

14
PROTECT YOURSELF

Copyright and trademark your titles, your content, your creations. Use an intellectual property attorney to help you figure out what you could and should do.

Do a web search when you're deciding what to call your business or workshop or presentation, so you're not infringing on someone else's trademark. And when you've come up with a good name, see if a domain name is available.

Creating your intellectual property is the hallmark of speaking and should not be taken lightly. All facets of your speech, from body of work to title, need to be protected on ethical as well as legal grounds. I've used ™ on all my titles, have copyrighted the bodies of my speeches and officially registered terms like Slip'em a Mikki ®.

15

"SOCIAL" MARKET RESEARCH – LEARNING ABOUT ANY INDUSTRY

There's a great way to learn about any industry: Using LinkedIn Groups. I do this every time I land a client in an industry I've not served before. Or when I'm pursuing a new prospect in the same situation. Marketing and sales professionals, listen up!

When I signed a new client in the digital printing business, I joined the "Digital Printing" group in LinkedIn (use the Groups Directory function to search for relevant words or phrases). Not only does the Digital Printing group have roughly 100,000 members, but there are also subgroups for specialties including Wide Format printing, Label printing and such. In the main group alone there are 250 discussions ongoing right now – on the important issues and opportunities of the day.

By reviewing these discussion threads you can learn about the industry at a hyper-accelerated rate. In essence you're learning from 100,000 brains rather than just your own. You can post a question and get answers directly from these people. If you're thinking about offering a new product or service, why not ask them for their input before making your investment. And when they post a question for which you have an answer, you have an invaluable opportunity to display your expertise and increase your visibility. This is selling by attracting them to you! It's a magnet instead of a hammer.

There are a variety of other ways to benefit from LinkedIn Groups. If you're running a not-for-profit organization and want to learn how to most effectively use social media, why not join a LinkedIn Group called "Social Media Today" and post a question:

"Does anyone have best practice examples of how not-for-profits are using social media?"

In fact, someone already posted this question and there are over 300 answers ready for your review.

Indeed, none of us is as smart as all of us!

16
TEMPLATE

Here's the template for every speech I give:

- **Opening**
  Open with a question, a quote, a story, a statistic (make it a provocative one), a name, date or place, a video...

- **Objectives**
  Often substituted with the words *intentions* or *promises* – typically 3-5, depending on the length of the speech. This gives an audience a road map of how you will use their valuable time and will set expectations for your content.

- **Story-Point-Takeaway**
  Most good storytellers stop after they make a point. The great storytellers provide the takeaway or the CTA (call to action). Without that your story becomes a *so what*? Remember, they're listening for the WIIFM, *what's in it for me.*

- **Repeat**
  Repeat the format of Story-Point-Takeaway as many times as the number of stories in your speech, or the length of your speech allows.

- **Restate**

  Restate your objectives so the audience knows that you've kept your promises and met your objectives.

- **Closing**

  Choose from the same list of possible openings. They can be the same or different, for example you can open with a question and close with a quote or vice versa.

17
WHAT'S UP WITH ALL THESE PEOPLE ENDORSING YOUR SKILLS?

On May 5, 2016 LinkedIn celebrated its 13th birthday. It now has roughly half a billion users, a quarter of whom are in the United States. Every second, two more professionals join LinkedIn. So what's up with all these people suddenly endorsing your skills?

I'm not talking about the "Recommendations." LinkedIn has had that feature since the early days and it's rarely used, except when someone's looking for a job and asks someone else to write a recommendation for them.

No, I'm talking about the "Skills Endorsements" added more recently. It seems as if every day someone new is endorsing me (and probably you). I think this feature is a great addition to LinkedIn although many users are still confused by it.

Here's why it's important: When somebody signs up for LinkedIn, they're asked to list their skills. You may not remember doing this yourself because it was a day-one activity, not repeated thereafter. The problem with the collective lists of our skills is that they're all self-reported. In a world where resume padding is legendary (remember the CEO who Yahoo quickly hired and then fired?), how valuable is a self-reported list?

Whenever someone views your profile, LinkedIn poses a question: "Does [your name here] have these skills or expertise?" LinkedIn then presents five randomly selected skills from among those you claimed, offering the viewer the opportunity to "endorse" or "skip" any or all.

Think about it. A given associate may not have a full view of your skills, but when everybody provides input, the collective feedback is likely to be on target.

What am I more likely to believe about you, the skills that you claim or what everyone else says?

See how this makes LinkedIn's personnel data more valuable?

Addressing one other mystery, I've frequently heard people say, "There's no way that Jane Smith would have viewed my profile." Indeed, she may not have, but if she viewed and endorsed someone else's profile, LinkedIn then displayed four of her connections listing one skill for each and asked "What skills or expertise do your other connections have?"

So be careful with whom you link. Hint: Stick to people you know and respect professionally. That's what LinkedIn advises.

You might want to review your own profile. What does the world say about you? For that matter, what does the world say about your potential customer or potential employee?

That could be even more valuable to know.

18
CUSTOMIZING YOUR TOPIC

Customize your topic to the theme of the conference or industry you're speaking to.

Customer-izing™ is not as difficult as it may sound and is actually quite interesting and fun for the speaker.

Send a questionnaire to your client with all the information you'd like to gather for your presentation. Perhaps it's knowing who their competition is or what the latest project or challenges are. Learn people's names, incidents in the past, anecdotes about the industry, some humor about attendees (that has been cleared and approved to use).

Research the jargon and history of the industry as well as the corporate culture. Try to make it *their* speech, *their* topic. You don't have to create a whole new speech; a little tweak here and there will help you to connect to that specific audience and make them feel you are connected to them and their industry.

19
FINDING THE BEST EMPLOYEES

LinkedIn.com allows you to do some amazing things when it comes to hiring. Even ignoring (and maybe you shouldn't) the premium recruiting features such as LinkedIn Recruiter, LinkedIn Job Posting, LinkedIn Career Page, and LinkedIn Talent Solutions, consider these two killer ideas:

First, the majority of us believe that the most talented people almost always have jobs unless they choose not to. Periodically, they transition directly from one position to another but they're rarely, if ever, "on the market" with their resumes posted on Monster, Dice or Craigslist. That's where the bottom 10% lives (sorry to be so harsh).

Why not proactively pursue the top 10%? As part of LinkedIn's basic (aka free) service there is a mode called "Advanced People Search." You can access this mode by clicking the "Advanced" button just to the right of the "Search" box that appears at the top every LinkedIn page.

I call this mode "Google for finding people." Notice that you can then search for prospective employees based on keywords, companies they've worked for (current or past), schools, job titles and more, all within a specified radius of a given ZIP or postal code.

Amazing!

Create a relevant search query and then proactively pursue the best and the brightest. If you save the query, you can even get automatic weekly updates as new people meet the criteria.

Second, most companies believe in reference checking. But if you get your references from your candidates, I've got a question for you: "What kind of sociopath can't gin up three good references?" If I give my brother some scotch and cigars, he'll say anything.

Traditional reference checking (those references that you get from your candidate) is a feel-good waste of time.

Instead, try what I call "blind" reference checking. LinkedIn used to provide "Reference Search" as a neatly packaged feature but discontinued it in June 2015. Given that it was one of their most valuable capabilities, my theory is that they saw some liability in providing it. Still, that shouldn't stop the rest of us from using Advanced People Search to find blind references.

Yes, it's a little more work but compare it to the cost of a bad hire, in time, money and pain? I recommend seeking permission from your candidates to do this. Not only will it help you avoid a lawsuit (yes, someone actually sued a company that used LinkedIn's now-discontinued Reference Search tool and then passed on hiring them), it will likely unmask the bad candidates up front.

"You're not comfortable with blind reference checking? Thanks for opting out of our process."

I'm not advocating doing anything that violates Affirmative Action, EEOC (the Equal Employment Opportunity Commission) or any other law or fairness principle. I'm simply suggesting that in the war for talent, you should give your company every advantage!

LinkedIn will get you there.

20
RESOURCEs

Use all resources to create and customize your presentations:

- Books
- Magazines
- MP3s
- Videos
- Industry publications
- Newsletters
- Podcasts
- Webinars
- vlogs
- blogs
- Google
- Google
- Google...

If I'm speaking for accountants, I'll do a Google search for "accountant facts," "accountant history," "accountant lingo," "accountant stories," "accountant quotes," "accountant humor..."

21

ESTABLISHING TRUST ... TO MAKE A CONNECTION (aka SALE)

Before you can sell your product or service, you must first discover your prospective customer's pain. And before a prospect will share that, you have to establish rapport (which works because it builds trust, the foundation for any transaction).

Social media helps you do this in so many ways; just pick your favorite. For example, before meeting with a new prospect, review their LinkedIn profile to identify possible connection points (a shared college, hobby, sport, past employer, industry association or professional acquaintance).

Recently, a Baltimore-based CEO told me his big break came when he discovered, using LinkedIn, that a tough prospect shared a background playing college lacrosse. After years of trying, that specific point of rapport opened the door and (no doubt after lots more hard work) ultimately led to a big sale.

When communicating to a larger audience, a current event or cultural touchstone can provide an equally effective connection point. For example, on their blog (read by roughly 15,000 airline industry executives), Boeing cleverly riffed on the 20th anniversary of the movie "Back to the Future" to explore the past and future of the airline industry. Not only did they make a connection, but in their post they "framed" their readers' (aka potential customers) thinking in a way that probably didn't help Airbus.

And for an important product launch, Microsoft did a humorous send-up of a YouTube video sensation (remember the Crazy Double Rainbow Guy?) to promote its Windows Live Photo Gallery product. People loved it and told their friends.

So next time you need to make a connection, try using social media to find a common point of rapport to get started.

22
BECOME AN EXPERT

Become an expert on a topic you're passionate about. If you love time management, read every book you can find on the subject, attend every presentation, and talk to as many people as you can. Include all the resources in your learning until you've mastered the subject enough to speak fluently and naturally about it.

It's very easy today to become the expert through the many online resources available. One I recommend is to watch TED talks; they can inspire topics or expertise you may not even realize you have, ones you can leverage through speaking.

Watch others who are experts in a field you're interested in and then don't adopt, but adapt to your own speaking style.

23
MARK ZUCKERBERG'S IMPORTANT OBSERVATION

Mark Zuckerberg, Facebook's founder, once wrote in a letter to his shareholders:

"We think a more open and connected world will help create a stronger economy with more authentic businesses that build better products and services. As people share more, they have access to more opinions from the people they trust about the products and services they use. This makes it easier to discover the best products and improve the quality and efficiency of their lives."

Notice the phrases "authentic businesses" and "opinions from people they trust." Think about this paragraph in total: It's a tectonic shift for business. Whether you sell to consumers, to other businesses, to governments or to not-for-profit organizations, it means information is flowing freely. It means there's no place to hide imperfections.

Whether Facebook (specifically) is the right tool for your business is irrelevant. In a social world, your business will succeed only if your products and services (including customer support) truly provide the best value in your industry.

In a world of perfect information, it's likely that only the best two players will survive (all markets require competition). If there are nine competitors in your space, random chance gives you a 20% possibility of being one of the two winners.

It's time to do an honest assessment. If your prospects and customers knew EVERYTHING about your organization and about all of your competitors, would they pick you? If not, it's time to start re-engineering your offerings, ideally involving your customers using an Idea Exchange from www.SalesForce.com or www.UserVoice.com.

It's time to enhance your customer support processes, ideally involving your customers using www.ZenDesk.com or www.GetSatisfaction.com.

And it's time to upgrade your corporate culture to attract and retain the best talent.

Indeed, if your culture and your recruiting practices are not the best among all your competitors, in a world of perfect information, who is going to work for you? Not the brightest, that's for sure (see www.GlassDoor.com to understand why).

With Facebook membership now larger than the population of any country (including China), a more open world is already upon us.

It's time to get your business ready.

24
LEADING EDGE

Take a leading-edge approach to your topic. If you want to inspire, do it with heart. If you want to provoke, be a contrarian. If you want to teach, see what's hot in the headlines.

And give it all your unique perspective.

25
THE RULE OF 1%

Early in 2014, Time Magazine Online reported that the "The Free-Marketing Gravy Train is Over on Facebook."

The beginning of the end started a few months earlier in October 2013. People were getting too many updates in their Facebook feeds, reportedly 1,500 per day. Even a millennial can't keep up with that many updates.

Facebook addressed the problem by introducing a feed-optimization scheme that presented users with just the "best" 20% of their updates. Guess who got the short end of that stick? Yes, our businesses.

Facebook was trying to solve a second problem at the same time. Their homepage says "It's free and always will be." But Facebook is a public company and needs to grow its revenues, and quickly. Guess where they're planning to get money? Yes, our businesses.

During the first month of Facebook's feed optimization program, your business posts received just 12% exposure. Four months later, the number was 6%. By July 2014, your "reach" was down to something approximating 1%. That means if you have 10,000 Likes on Facebook and post an update, roughly 100 of your fans will see it. Post every day for a month and by the end of that month, one-third of your fans will have seen one post and two-thirds will have seen none.

This is a crazy-inefficient way to talk to anyone. Twitter works the same way for a different reason. People aren't on Twitter most of the day. When they sign-on they look at what's happening now but not at what happened earlier or at what happens after they leave. Twitter's "Moments" feature is the latest attempt to address this issue. We'll see whether anything changes.

In either case, I call this the Rule of 1%. Just multiply your Likes or Followers by 1% and decide whether it's worth the effort you're putting into creating content for them.

No, the free versions of Facebook and Twitter are all but worthless.

To get around the Rule of 1% you have to pay, of course. My recommendation is to switch to other tools (say LinkedIn or Google+) or start experimenting with Facebook and/or Twitter advertising to learn how to generate a positive return on investment (ROI) for your business. You can target people using an amazing array of characteristics including location, demographics, interests, language, behaviors and more. And you can track conversions with a "conversion tracking pixel tool" so you'll know exactly how many conversions your ads are generating.

Things change. The free marketing gravy train may indeed be over on Facebook but that door closing may open a door to very profitable and measurable advertising for your business.

It's time to find out.

26
DOING IT BETTER

Study your competition. What are they doing? How are they doing it?

You don't want to copy them, you just want to be informed, and then do something better and more innovative.

Adapt, don't adopt!

27

AN IDEA EXCHANGE

One hundred years ago, I figure that most business people knew their customers' names, needs, likes and dislikes. Since then, we've scaled up in the name of productivity, volume and value. Along the way, we mastered the art of the monologue — think websites, product brochures, press releases, advertisements and email blasts — but lost the original customer intimacy.

Social networking tools allow us to create dialogue that reconnects us as individuals, helping to restore customer intimacy. One of my favorite such tools is an "idea exchange."

At www.MyStarbucksIdea.com, you can make a suggestion, vote on the ideas of others or see a list of Starbucks' changes resulting directly from customers' suggestions. Recently, I received an email from Starbucks saying, "Dave, here are the first 275 changes we've made based on your ideas!" (Note: Only 271 of the ideas were mine personally; a couple of other folks contributed, too).

If you've ever left Starbucks with a coffee in hand and the lid was sealed with a green stick, well, that was a customer idea. So was the reusable cup sleeve that's reducing landfill waste and lowering Starbucks' costs. We can all save the planet together.

Countless organizations are facilitating similar dialogues. Dell is learning with its customers at www.IdeaStorm.com. Vancouver government officials are garnering the best ideas from their citizens at www.Vancouver.UserVoice.com. What a fabulous development: Politicians actually listening to and acting on the collective wisdom of their constituents!

You can run your own idea exchange for roughly $100/month with a service from www.BrightIdea.com, www.JiveSoftware.com, www.SalesForce.com or www.UserVoice.com.

Together these folks power idea exchanges for more than 200,000 organizations, including all the examples I've cited here.

What are you waiting for?

28
BE YOU-NIQUE

"Anyone can copy different, no one can copy unique."

As examples, my web site has lips that open and close instead of a regular toolbar.

My media kit has a hologram of me on the cover.

These are unique to me and cannot be copied. *Different* would be just using various colors that everyone could copy.

Strive for the unique.

29

GLASSDOOR

If you've never heard of Glassdoor.com, all you need to know is that it's where your current employees, or more likely your former employees, and even possibly people who you interviewed but did not hire, go to review your company.

And you thought only hotels and restaurants had to worry about reviews.

I know a millennial (let's call him Jason) who had been in his first post-college job for more than two years (that's a long time if you're a millennial).

One day he got a call from a recruiter looking to interview him for a new position. Not surprisingly he said yes.

The interview went well and it seemed that an offer was on the way, so Jason did his due diligence on the potential employer. He checked them out on Glassdoor.com. Here's an actual excerpt from one of the first reviews:

"It's a very unstable company with abusive, arrogant management...[Y]ou are always working hard and staying late but still being screamed at about whatever crazy thing has upset the owner. He likes to hold unplanned meetings and single people out as 'morons'...It's a terrible place to work."

Jason raised the issue with the hiring manager. The manager raised the proposed starting salary by 30%. Again not surprisingly, Jason said yes, but here's the question: Do you want to pay a 30% premium to compensate for issues in your corporate culture?

Do you think that Jason will be at the new company for the long term? Would you blame him if he used the opportunity as a stepping stone?

Glassdoor can hurt you in another way as well, as their reviews often appear in top search results when someone Googles your organization's name.

A few Christmases ago, a friend of mine decided to gift his customers a cow. Well, not a cow to his customers, but a cow on their behalf to a family in the third world. You can do that with Heifer International. Except here is what my friend learned when Googling "Heifer International" and clicking on the fourth result (literally the first two sentences of the first review displayed on Glassdoor): "If only the donors that contribute to this organization knew what really happened behind the doors of the 'pretty building.' Especially with their money."

A little more Googling revealed a competitor, Oxfam, that was highly respected by its employees (more than 100 Glassdoor reviews averaging 4.1 on a 5-point scale). So the family got their cow but not through Heifer International.

Indeed, a more open world is already upon us.

It's time to get your business ready.

30
FIND YOUR VOICE

Pay attention!

Study other speakers' styles. Take notes on what you like and don't like about their presentations, their style, their delivery.

Pay attention to when the audience is really engaged with them; when they get an unexpected laugh or ask a question that sparks a conversation.

Pay attention to people's reactions to various parts of their speech and use all that great information to help you develop your own speech and your own style.

This is how you find your voice.

31
TRAVEL APPS

While I don't have an objective measure to prove it, I believe I am at least twice as productive as I was five years ago because of the various apps I use on my smartphone and tablet. I'm constantly surprised at how many business owners haven't yet embraced this amazing new technology.

Here's a typical example of how I use apps for improved productivity, in this case for travel:

Yesterday, I did morning and afternoon keynote presentations for groups in Houston, TX. At 4:00 pm, as I headed out into the unbelievable Houston rush hour traffic using Uber (a transportation app) to the airport, my TripIt app told me my flight was cancelled. This was a serious problem. I had to be in Canton, Ohio by morning or I'd miss my next speaking engagement.

I fire up my FlightBoard app which shows every flight out of Houston during the next four hours. I see that Delta has a 5:50 pm departure running 15 minutes behind schedule and I can make that because Waze (my social GPS app) has a deadly reliable estimate of my arrival time at IAH (5:03 pm, in case you're curious).

I fire up my Kayak app and discover that the Delta flight to Pittsburgh (via Atlanta) is available for less than $200. I buy the ticket and then launch my Delta app to get my boarding passes. I add these to my Apple Wallet app so they'll be available on my Apple Watch when I reach the airport.

I board my Delta flight bound for Atlanta and we pull back from the gate 15 minutes late as projected. Unfortunately, within one minute the pilot stops the plane and shuts down the engines. I can't help but remember that DELTA is an acronym that stands for

Doesn't Ever Leave The Airport, but this time it's not actually their fault. It's a thunderstorm that has the entire airport under a ground stop.

Finally the lightning passes and we take off to Atlanta. As soon as the wheels touch down, I switch my iPhone out of "airplane mode" and receive a TripIt update. I'll transcribe it for you here:

TripIt Pro [10:00 PM]: DL54 arr term N, gate E-35. 8m to make conn @ ATL DL1072 term N, gate E-16.

In short, I've got 8 minutes to make my connection. Did I mention that I'm sitting at the very back of the plane because I purchased my ticket just 90-minutes before departure?

FlightBoard also tells me that the Pittsburgh flight is indeed leaving in 8 minutes but upon finally disembarking, I run to gate E-16 anyway. Not surprisingly, when I get there the gate area is deserted save for one friendly agent who says, "Man, I held it for you as long as I could." I'm sure it wasn't even close.

So now I call my travel agent's emergency 24-hour hotline for help. According to the agent, the next flight to Pittsburgh, Akron, Cleveland or anywhere close departs Atlanta at 8:30 am tomorrow. This is really bad news as my 3-hour keynote in Canton is scheduled to start at 8:00 am. I'll miss it entirely.

So back to FlightBoard. Miracle! It's now 10:20 pm but the 10:04 pm Delta flight to Cleveland is showing a 60-minute delay. My travel agent can't see it (or book it) in her system because it's past departure time. FlightBoard shows the gate is B3. While I've got plenty of time to make it there I run anyway. Long story short, I make the flight with time to spare. I'm the only guy on the plane who's happy that it's running behind schedule.

Before we take off, I use the Hertz app to book a car in Cleveland and the Marriot app to book a Springfield Suites hotel in Akron. My Google Maps app shows that the hotel is roughly two-thirds of the way along the preferred route to my meeting in Canton, so I'll have just a 30-minute drive in the morning.

Five years ago this happy ending would have been impossible. Embrace your apps, business people!

32
MIND MAPPING

Use Mind Mapping as a technique to develop your topic and your target audiences.

Begin with a topic or idea and branch out from there with single words that relate to that central core. Then, branch out from there with words that expand further on those ideas.

This helps to develop your overall theme and elaborate on it. Include images and/or graphics if that helps flesh out your concept.

Try using this graphic and see where it takes you. As an example, put Healthcare in the center for your industry or expertise. In the outer circles add your secondary and tertiary industries, i.e. doctors – specialties; nurses – associations, pharmacists, etc.

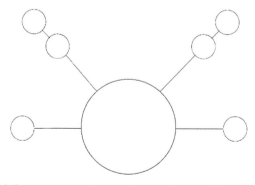

Or look for some mind mapping software. iThoughts is an excellent mind mapping app (rated 4.5 stars).

33
PROMOTE THE POSITIVE (REVIEWS)

Have you noticed the proliferation of consumer review sites? It's not just Yelp (restaurants, etc.), TripAdvisor (hotels, etc.), and Angie's List (contractors, etc.). It's Amazon (everything they sell), Glassdoor (companies and employers) and Google (literally everything)!

The problem is that when we're unhappy about something we tell three times more people than when we're happy. And now we've got megaphones to do it. Combine this with another fact: We find what our peers say about your business to be 5- to 10-times more believable than anything you say. I have two suggestions:

1. Accept that information is flowing freely. As such, our businesses have to be better than in the past: more tuned in, more customer-focused, more responsive to complaints and even gentler on employees being terminated.
2. Social media helps great businesses succeed faster and helps poor businesses get out of business. Said another way, be better or be bankrupt.
3. Now, assuming that your business is doing everything right, why not promote the positive?

Recently I dined in a delightful crab place in Charleston, South Carolina. After I complimented my server and left a nice tip, she handed me a card. This card was not in general circulation in the restaurant. Rather, she was trained to present this card to anyone who appeared to be thrilled with their meal. Do you want to know what the card said?

"Please allow others to know about your wonderful dining experience by posting on Yelp, Fodors, 10Best, TripAdvisor or Yahoo's TravelGuide. Thank you."

There was no incentive and no reward. However, when someone does something nice for us (including providing a tasty meal, expertly served), we want to reciprocate. Think about how you use this simple idea to drive more positive conversation about your business. Could you get your happiest customers to write reviews? Could you get your happiest employees to go on Glassdoor?

Now you're thinking!

34

YOUR EXPERTISE

Draw upon your expertise. Develop that expertise and then apply it laterally to bridge to other companies or industries. Then think of who needs your information and how you find that particular audience.

As an example, you might be an expert in leadership. Your topic would be embraced by CEOs and you speak for Vistage Worldwide.

You leverage that by thinking: If your topic is relevant to a company at the managerial level, it could appeal to any internal or external board of directors.

In this way you can penetrate an organization vertically. If you were to approach it laterally, you would look for companies and trade associations that would also be interested in aspects of this broad topic by breaking it down into sub-topics or groups.

35
YOUTUBE (FOR VIDEO CUSTOMER TESTIMONIALS)

In business, we've long utilized customer testimonials to help us attract new prospects. Typically we've done it in text form but how convincing is that? Anybody could have written or edited it. And text does little to convey emotion and enthusiasm.

Even so, we rely on written customer testimonials because we know that what others say about us is more credible than what we say about ourselves.

What if your prospects could see your customers talking about you in a video? Social is increasingly about video. And YouTube (the leading video site) long ago passed Yahoo and Bing as the number two search engine (behind Google itself, YouTube's owner).

People don't want to hear your customers saying how awesome you are. Instead, your prospects want to hear about what your customers have accomplished using your products and services. Remember, in marketing it's not about you, it's about them, their objectives, and their customers.

You don't need to hire a video production company because you're not looking to make a commercial. We've all seen plenty of those and we know how to tune them out. Instead, grab your Android or iPhone and get with your best customers. Or find them at tradeshows or industry events where there's energy in the air and many of them in attendance.

In either case you'll have authenticity working for you. Ask your customer to talk for 15 seconds about their situation before doing business with you. They'll describe the same pain that your top prospects are experiencing. Then have your customer talk for

45 seconds about what they've been able to achieve using your products and services. They'll paint the same beautiful bridge that you want your prospects to cross.

With your smartphone in hand, stand just 3 to 4 feet away from the person, framing their head and shoulders with the camera at eye height. This makes it feel like we're face-to-face with the person, increasing trust. Avoid windows and bright backgrounds. You don't want your customer to appear to be in the witness protection program.

And be sure to hold the smartphone in the horizontal orientation. Holding it vertically results in black bars on both sides of a computer screen or monitor (so called "vertical video syndrome").

36
A UNIQUE PERSPECTIVE

Find a different perspective by looking at your expertise and asking yourself, "What if I reversed my opinion or idea to come from the positive/negative side to help people?"

Explore topics as they relate to the specific issues of the times.

An example would be writing about the benefits of social media in our world today as Dave does so eloquently. Someone else might write about how it's adversely affected our lives.

Every topic can be aligned with the good, the bad, and the ugly. Look at the current magazine and newspaper headlines and ask yourself "what if" questions to come up with that unique perspective.

37
MILLIONS OF MILLENIALS

I heard recently that the Millennials, the group born between 1982 and 2000, also referred to as Gen Y, will make up 49% of the workforce by 2020. That's essentially half of your employees and half of your customers.

To get a view of what that would look like, consider that the Millennials already represent the majority of business travelers!

Gen Y is a huge group (79 million Americans), making its size on par with the Baby Boomers. Gen X, which came in between (sandwich anyone?), is substantially smaller.

Throw in the fact that younger people are more willing to travel (fewer family commitments, greater zest for adventure, etc.) and you get the picture. This demographic development has travel-related companies scrambling to redefine their services.

In response, Hilton started allowing travelers to check in via smartphone, pick their own rooms from floor plan maps and then use their smartphones as their room keys.

OMG @Hilton #epic #justsayin' (In other words, "It sounds good to me.")

Meanwhile, a website called Airbnb has turned our homes into hotels. In just nine years, Airbnb has achieved a market cap exceeding Hilton and Marriott. At the same time, Uber (ridesharing) has become the world's most valuable private tech company.

The Millennials are changing everything. If you're not currently re-engineering your products, your corporate culture, your mobile-first website, your social media programs and your company's apps, well, you may not be in business tomorrow.

Consider this chapter to be your big wake-up call. Follow Hilton's lead ASAP. It's time to embrace the Millennials and learn to serve them, before your competitors do.

38
WHO CARES?

Get out a sheet of paper and, at the top write, "Who Cares?"

Under that write down your topic. Under that write down how many different types of people and industries to whom you can customize that topic.

So let's say your topic is, "How to Develop Self-Esteem." You could speak to teenagers, salespeople, managers, teachers, stay-at-home moms, college graduates, entrepreneurs...

If you speak on networking, perhaps you could target salespeople, insurance agents, marketing specialists.

In one instance I was coaching a woman who spoke at The Learning Annex on The Art of Flirting. She wanted to develop a corporate audience.

Who cares? Not that corporate audience! But we didn't have to throw the baby out with the bath water. We took her topic expertise and worked on it until it became about relationships, which could encompass business as well as personal, and then it fit right into the new audience she was targeting.

Use your imagination!

39
IMPROVED TEAM COLLABORATION

Here's something to think about: You and all of your company's employees spend on average a little more than 40% of your time working email. Is there anything in business that consumes 40% of your resources that you've never tried to optimize?

Here's another thing to consider: None other than Bill Gates is predicting that social networking apps will become ubiquitous in the workplace and will likely replace email as the dominant form of corporate communications.

Email is essentially the same technology that I first experienced when I joined Bell Labs in 1982. And so I've supplemented it with Dropbox, Evernote, Wunderlist, and texting on my MacBook Pro, iPad, iPhone, Apple Watch and "the cloud."

Is it perhaps time to say goodbye to email? Absolutely! Instead, say hello to Slack. First, know that Slack is funded by a veritable Silicon Valley dream team comprised of Andreessen Horowitz, Kleiner Perkins and Google Ventures. It doesn't get any better than that.

The Slack product was launched in 2013 and according-to-Wikipedia-so-it-must-be-true, attracted 8,000 customers in the first 24 hours. Hopefully none of these companies (or the hoards that came afterwards) are your competitors.

Is it that surprising that a small team of smart coders could create a system that's actually better for employee collaboration than email more than half a century later?

So what is Slack? It's private group texting (among employees), combined with integrated document sharing, synchronized across all your devices. If that sounds interesting, find a few volunteers in your organization to run a small-scale trial among themselves.

Not to be too stereotypical but they probably won't be the employees who were using email back in 1982. It's a good bet that they weren't even born yet in 1982.

After 30 days, have them report on the pros and cons of Slack vs. email. If the cons outweigh the pros, fail fast and keep an eye out for the next big thing.

But my guess is that the pros will prevail and your competitors will hate me.

But your employees won't.

40

TO POWERPOINT OR NOT TO POWERPOINT

If you use PowerPoint, follow the 10-20-30 rule:

- 10 slides
- 20 minutes
- 30-point font

And...

- Use a graphic, cartoon or photo on every slide
- No more than seven words per slide, upper and lower case
- Two to three colors per slide, no more
- PowerPoint should enhance your presentation not BE your presentation!

If you have a lot of text on your slides your audience will be reading the slides and not listening to you.

The worst: people who read aloud to the audience exactly what's on the screen. Just put your key points on the slides and then expound on them in an organic way, so those folks have a reason to keep listening.

41
YAMMER AND CHATTER

Millennials rarely, if ever, use e-mail. Why? With their fresh eyes, they've found social media tools that are more efficient and more effective for communicating. When they want to convey time-critical information, they send text messages. Otherwise they use a rich information-sharing cloud called Facebook.

While these tools are great for personal communication, what if we could use similar mechanisms for employee communication in our businesses? And we can.

For group texting, I'm talking about Microsoft Yammer or SalesForce.com Chatter. For document sharing I'm talking about Microsoft SharePoint and Office 365, or SalesForce.com's cloud-based customer relationship management (CRM) solution.

If you're already a happy customer of either Microsoft or Salesforce.com, you'll likely want to use these systems rather than Slack. Companies that have adopted such tools are experiencing a 30% reduction in e-mail.

Think about it: That amounts to one hour per day per employee for every person in your company. Some of that time will go towards the new tools, but not all of it. At the same time, businesses are achieving 52% faster access to information and holding 27% fewer meetings.

With Yammer or Chatter, there's an obvious difference compared to e-mail: Messages are concise (140 characters), so employees can determine with a glance whether an issue is important to them or not. Group texting is actually less distracting than email. And it's a closed private network with no outside noise and no spam.

Email is 70% spam.

Further, with Yammer or Chatter, information is no longer fragmented across individual employees' inboxes. Instead all messages (and linked documents) are part of a shared knowledge base searchable on demand today or years from now. Further, it's no longer the content producers who decide who consumes information via "To" "CC" and "BCC" fields. Instead, content consumers decide who to follow.

That's a 180-degree paradigm flip. Think about the implications of making it culturally illegal in your company to send documents via e-mail. Instead, post your documents to your cloud and text the associated links. When an employee leaves, you won't lose the corporate knowledge that would otherwise be in their e-mail archive and personal hierarchical (i.e., PC folder-based) filing system.

When new employees join, they'll get access to an existing corporate knowledge base instead of starting with a blank computer.

Like telegrams, pagers and fax machines, e-mail is now past its prime. It's time to equip your organization with the latest tools to improve employee communication and collaboration.

Before your competitors do.

42
'EVERYBODY' DOESN'T WORK

'Everybody' is not an audience. People who say they can talk on any subject to any audience are not focused on their marketing or goals.

Narrow down your topics to the industries and organizations that would be particularly interested in those specific topics and who would benefit most. Those are the ones who would be willing and able to pay. Then work from the local level to the national level.

Decide if you want to have a niche industry or a niche topic, or if you want to be a generalist.

I started as a generalist with a topic that had broad appeal and did not target any particular industry. Then I paid attention to the industries that "niched" me. It's a lot easier to get work, to get your fee in areas where your topic, style or expertise has perceived value.

43
DON'T LET YOUR BUSINESS GET UBER'D

Much of this book is about social media and social networking for business. However, this chapter is about apps. What do these two technologies have in common? In both cases, they're tools that are more efficient for some of our communication challenges. In speaking to tens of thousands of business executives around the United States each year, I find a surprising percentage are not embracing new technology, specifically tablets (think iPad or Surface Pro), smartphones (think iPhone or Android) and literally millions of apps. This is an incredibly dangerous, head-in-sand strategy.

Remember what Darwin observed: "It's not the strongest or most intelligent who survive, but those who adapt to a changing environment most quickly."

While it's true for species, it's true for businesses on a hyper-accelerated time scale. Think about it: How long can you stand still and not respond to your competition, not enhance your products and services, not upgrade your technology and team? It's impossible to keep up in business without thoroughly embracing technology.

If you're uncomfortable with technology, it's time to re-examine your mindset. Yes, it is just a mindset.

Start by getting your hands on some apps, just like a 4-year-old would. I have a few app recommendations for business:

For social media try one or more of the following: LinkedIn, Pulse (part of LinkedIn), Slack, Google+ and Hangouts (part of Google+).

But expand your horizons. If you travel at all, add Waze, TripIt, TripAdvisor and Yelp!

Also consider an app called Evernote that stores your notes and a vast array of other information in the cloud. It's my second brain! It works on all platforms and keeps everything in synch. You can put anything into Evernote and then find it fast wherever you are, whenever you need it.

While the basic version of Evernote is free, with the $70/year premium service you get optical character recognition (OCR). Imagine photographing a business card or scanning a document and finding it later based on the words it contains. Amazingly, Evernote can even recognize handwriting. You can even search for content based on where you were when you created it (location-based retrieval). It's a business productivity game-changer.

Here's the bottom line: If your competition is using tablets, apps and smartphones and you're not, you're at an increasing disadvantage. Like the dinosaurs, your business is not long for this planet. Adapt or die.

Don't let your business get Uber'd.

44
MAKING CONNECTIONS

Understand the demographics of your audience: age, gender, education, income, etc.

More importantly, understand the psychographics, i.e. what are their aspirations, their attitudes, their habits? What books do they read? What music do they listen to? Where do they travel?

Consider ethnographies, the culture of organizations.

Once you know the demographics, psychographics and ethnographies, it becomes easier to use their industry jargon, play to their specific needs and customize your entire presentation so it sounds like you work in their industry, even if you don't. Audiences appreciate this and will invite you back.

The better you know your audience, the easier it will be to connect with them.

45

UNLIKE THE ROLLING STONES, YOU CAN GET SATISFACTION

Every few years a company establishes its name and undying customer loyalty by providing unbelievable customer service. If you've ever dealt with Nordstrom (department stores), you know the experience. Others in this wonderful category include L.L. Bean, Four Seasons Hotels, Apple, Starbucks and Lexus. And of course, Zappos.

Zappos is an Internet retailer that sells shoes. That's the one thing that should be all but impossible to sell on the Internet. Have you ever purchased shoes without trying them on?

To solve this problem, Zappos adopted an insane customer service model. No matter what you buy, shipping is always free (no minimum). And so is return shipping. No questions asked. No hassles, ever.

You can, for example, order three different sizes of a given shoe and keep just the one pair that fits best. You have up to 365 days to return the other two pairs. You can even return all three pairs.

If by chance you purchase something on February 29 (leap day), you have until the next leap day to return it. That's an unbelievable four years. Like I said, insane.

Zappos' CEO Tony Hseih recently revealed a key component of their formula. It's something that 100,000+ other businesses are now doing to improve their own customer service.

Zappos' not-so-secret weapon is a "cloud-based" tool called "Get Satisfaction". This social software allows you to create a community of customers. In short, it's a new social media form of the traditional customer support forum. But it's more than that. It's the ultimate embodiment of "the wisdom of crowds" meets "knowledge capture and reuse."

According to Hseih, "There's a simple reason that we were one of the first to raise our hands at Zappos and start using Get Satisfaction: A lot of our approach to making people happy with timely, human customer service is already baked into this product. They get it."

"GetSat," as fans call it, allows your customers to type their questions in natural language. As they type, GetSat (and alternative products like Zendesk) uses auto-complete (like Google does in search) to suggest relevant questions for which it already has answers. While you can see the leverage in that, it gets better. If the user doesn't find a relevant question and answer, he or she can post the question for other customers to answer.

It turns out that people like to share what they know, either to show that they're smart or to be helpful. Either way they're answering your technical support questions for free. Your team simply reviews the proposed answers and approves them, rejects them, or modifies them for accuracy. Thus, customers and your support team share answers, ideas and solutions. This decreases the load on your support team and more importantly, you tap into the power of "none of us is as smart as all of us."

Companies that use GetSat report on average:

- 89% reduction in customer support load (that's a 10X gain!)
- Increased sense of customer community (after all, it's the happiest, most knowledgeable fellow customers who participate)
- Improved customer satisfaction scores

What's not to love? You can reduce your costs and get better results. And you'll be following the same customer service excellence approach as Zappos.

Yes, social media tools can actually save you more time and money than they consume, and improve results.

Get Satisfaction proves it.

46
READY, SET...GOALS

Do you want to speak only locally or do you want to speak nationally? Maybe you want to speak internationally.

Those decisions could affect your topic or target audience. Set speaking goals if you aspire to do this professionally.

How much income do you want from speaking? How often do you want to speak? Do you want to earn your CSP (Certified Speaking Professional certification)?

Your goals can be as simple as mine were when I first started. I had three five-year goals:

1. To speak internationally
2. To earn my CSP
3. To make a six-figure income

After I set those goals, I created the "how."

To achieve the international goal I knew I had to find opportunities either with companies that had overseas branches or associations with international members. For me, Million Dollar Round Table was the key that catapulted me into worldwide speaking, which I did my first three years.

For goal number two, one must wait five years to apply for CSP certification, and meet certain criteria in terms of number of clients, fee totals, etc.

The income goal was easy in the sense that I knew how many presentations I had to give at my then-current fee to hit my financial target.

47
ESP USING SOCIAL MEDIA

You've heard of Twitter. More than 500 million times a day people share whatever's on their mind using 140 characters or less. In total, it's fair to call it random noise. But what if you could listen for information relevant to your business, maybe just in your geographic area?

Well, you can at www.twitter.com/search-home!

Let's say you run a car dealership in Mars (PA, that is). Let's find out who wants a new car right now!

In the Twitter search box type: "new car" (in quotes to search for the entire phrase). And since you serve a limited geographic area, add "near:16046" (without quotes). To be more specific add "within: 25mi" (without quotes) because people will drive only so far for a good deal. Yes, the Internet and cell phones know precisely where we are; scary but true.

1.93 seconds later you'll see local folks with new cars on their minds:

- "MY NEW CAR IS GONNA BE A 2017 CAR"
- "Scramble and find a new car - my inspection is up and costs way too much to fix. 188k!"
- "I wanna New Car!!!"
- "It's time for a new car!"

For each of these Tweeters you might begin a conversation by offering a "secret discount code" or helpful advice such as: "I'm a car dealer. You always get a better deal when you…" Place the @ sign in front of their username and they'll almost certainly see your response.

One other thing: Once you've created a search query that works, you never have to do it again. Use a Twitter tool called Tweetdeck and you'll receive automatic notifications as new matches occur.

How cool is that?

48
THAT SOUNDS INTERESTING!

The title of your presentation is as important as your content. It's the first impression you make when you tell people what you speak about. Your title sets up an expectation, it has an implication, it plants a seed in the listener's mind.

The accepted rule in the industry is that your title should plainly say: When you hear this you will discover how to _____ so that you can _____.

That's one way to think about it.

Here's another:

I became an accidental 'brand' because I paid attention to how people remembered me (my hair, my clothes, my style, the colors I identified with...) and then I exploited those unique factors. To stay true to my brand I have always created titles that fit my outrageousness.

A few of my titles are: Speak Loudly and Carry a Big Shtick™, Your Goal-den Opportunities™, Your Network Is Important to Your Net Worth™.

When someone hears your title you want them to say, "Oh! Now THAT sounds interesting!"

49
YOUR OWN SOCIAL NETWORK (NING)

Have you ever thought about building your own social network tailored to your specific purpose? It could be public or private and you'd be entirely in control. Such a community could be a more effective, more efficient means of communicating among a group, significantly reducing email, phone calls and missed opportunities.

Cost and complexity are no longer blocking factors in creating a social network. You can create an open or closed Ning group in about 30 minutes at a cost of not millions of dollars but just $25 per month. That's not per member; that covers up to 1,000 members. And a group of 10,000 members is just $49 per month.

Imagine having a fully customized Facebook-like community for connecting your key customers and prospects, your employees (private, controlled membership) or your partners and suppliers.

A Ning community can include blogs (and associated RSS feeds), sub-groups, photos, videos, documents and much, much more. And unlike most other forms of social networking, Ning can be entirely under your control- or not.

In addition to its enhanced communication benefits, Ning can also be a knowledge repository for sharing documents, spreadsheets, and presentations while keeping them permanently accessible. If you have a distributed team and this sounds like an improvement to your current communication and collaboration approach, checkout www.ning.com.

50
BUTTERFLIES

Even the most seasoned speakers get butterflies sometimes.

The best defense against butterflies is knowing your speech backwards and forwards. Practice, practice, practice! There's no better method.

When you really know your material, you're more relaxed and you have more fun with your audience.

Deep breathing before you go in front of your audience helps too. When we're nervous, our breathing gets constricted so we need to get oxygen into our lungs.

Before your presentation greet attendees, interact with people...laugh! Stay busy.

And never, ever use a script. No one wants a speaker to read to them.

Instead, write your keywords on a sheet of paper that you can put on the lectern or a table in case you need to refer to it. Never use index cards – it's too easy to drop them or get them out of order.

It's perfectly okay to go to the podium with notes to scan. It's not okay to read notes or memorize a script – it'll sound canned and you'll lose your connection to the audience.

51
SOCIAL APPS

Most people didn't notice when it happened in the fourth quarter of 2010.

Yes, it was that long ago that smartphone and tablet sales surpassed desktop and notebook computer sales in unit volume.

Since then, the gap has widened dramatically. The last time I checked www.internetlivestats.com, mobile devices were out-selling traditional computers by 11-to-1. Astounding!

Which raises a question: What's the best way to connect with your employees, your business partners and your customers?

Yesterday the answer was by deploying a website. Today, the best answer may be by providing apps.

If this is all new to you, a great way to get a feel for things is by exploring some social apps. Go to your favorite app store and find at least one mobile social app and add it to your phone. The list of choices is long (and growing), including: Facebook, Twitter, Foursquare, Google+, Instagram, LinkedIn, Snapchat, Twitter, Yelp and TripAdvisor, to name just a few.

If you have no experience with any of these here's my recommendation for the first two to try:

1. LinkedIn – the professional's social network. LinkedIn now has roughly half a billion members worldwide. Because it's tied to our professional careers, it's likely to be the one social network/app that will stand the test of time. You'll discover that it unlocks an amazing network of second connections (people that your

professional associates know), roughly 500 times more people than you know directly.

2. Yelp – a foodie's nirvana. It's no longer about the Zagat Guide and local newspaper reviews. Now it's about what *they* say – *they* being past customers of any given restaurant. I travel almost every week and almost never have a bad meal because I let the Yelpers guide me. They're fabulous.

As you experience these social apps on your smartphone, start thinking about how you might engage your target audiences: your employees, your customers and other important groups.

Perhaps you'll do it using one or more of these mobile social apps. Or maybe you'll build an app of your own.

In the past, we put a lot of thought into our Internet presence and search engine optimization. Now it's time to shift our thinking (and some of our resources) to the post-PC world.

52
LIKEABILITY FACTORS

What are the likeability factors that get an audience on your side in the FIRST MINUTES?

Use humor in your presentation. Use names of some of the audience members, or industry jargon or inside information, all of which are garnered from a pre-interview with the insiders or event planners.

Smile, make eye contact throughout, use humor. Get them involved with some kind of interaction, like having them raise a hand in answer to a question, or giving them a directive to write something, or to turn to their neighbor and share something, etc.

Roughly every seven minutes, do something to change their physicality.

Keep them on their toes and awake!

53
RESPONSIVE DESIGN

So you agree about the importance of mobile technology and Apps, given that sales of tablets (aka iPads) and smartphones exceed sales of traditional computers (desktops and notebooks).

But what happens when someone visits your existing blog or website using a mobile device? If they're on a smartphone (in other words, viewing a 4" – 5" screen), it's a good bet that they won't be delighted by your microscopic text.

To fix that for every possible device, all you need to do is to update your website/blog using "responsive design." You don't need to know the technical details – just be sure to use these two specific words when directing your web designer. With responsive design, your website responds to the number of horizontal pixels (aka screen width) available to each visitor.

If they're in front of a 22" monitor, that's one thing. If their browser is sized to just half that screen, it's another. If their iPad is in landscape mode and they rotate it 90 degrees, that's two other things. And their smartphone can be two more.

Regardless of screen width, responsive design ensures that text is presented in a readable font size, wrapping as necessary at the edges of the screen.

Top-level menus that are too wide become drop-downs.

Videos use the full screen width, whatever it is.

Next time you redesign your website, hire a designer who's mastered responsive design.

If they can do it entirely on WordPress (a content management system that is as easy to edit as Microsoft Word), all the better. You'll have a website that works on every device, even the new ones to be released tomorrow, and you'll be able to manage the content yourself.

54
THE AHA!

Stories have structure. They need a protagonist and an antagonist. The protagonist is the hero of the story. The antagonist is the person or thing that keeps the hero from reaching his/her goal.

Stories have a beginning, middle and end, not beginning, muddle and end. There must be an arc that keeps us intrigued, takes us on a journey, and keeps us interested.

Eventually there is an incident which changes the course of the story and allows the hero to overcome the obstacles and succeed.

That's when we hear the WIIFM – what's-in-it-for-me factor – or, as I call it, the aha!

55
WHERE INTERNET TRAFFIC COMES FROM

There's one reason Google is among the most valuable and important companies on the planet. For an instant, many times each day, Google knows exactly what's on your mind. And then they deliver an almost infinite number of relevant results instantly.

Not that you care about more than the first twenty listings (or need to) because they're that good.

But did you ever wonder where your own website's traffic comes from? Would you like to know how many visitors arrive directly, or from a search, or from another website (aka a "referral")? Or would you like to know what devices people use when visiting your site (say smartphone vs. desktop vs. tablet). Or what pages they spend the most time on?

Not surprisingly, Google can tell you all this and more. Just activate their fabulous free tool called "Google Analytics" for your website and/or blog and you'll gain incredible insights into how many people are visiting you and why.

But what if you could know this about your competition? Then you would know who to keep an eye on, whose digital marketing initiatives are most effective, who to "copy".

Let others succeed or fail with their early experiments. Go to www.Alexa.com (an Amazon company) and enter your competitor's web address. Prepare to be amazed! You'll see their global traffic rank (even for low volume sites), 6 months of traffic history, the top five referring sites, the top five search terms (keywords) and even the demographics of their visitors (gender, education level, and browsing location).

You can use this knowledge about their most effective keywords if they're relevant to your business too! Confirm, using Google's Keyword Planner tool, that the keywords are being searched at a compelling volume in your geographic region. Then, produce good quality content around those topics (blog posts, landing pages, etc.).

You can bet that if it's working for them, it will work for you too.

56
DATA WITH SOUL

Brene Brown said, "Storytelling is data with soul." Stories don't tell us how to think, they give us something to think about.

We place ourselves in other people's stories if we're engaged, and that's based on our own experiences. It's why we go to the movies and to plays. It's why we read books. We want to relate to the storyteller and what's happening in the narrative.

Stories move us to action, data does not. Stories create an emotion, data does not. If you must share data, wrap it in a story.

You live stories every day. Keep a story journal and every time you remember one, every time you create one, write it down.

Be relatable – tell a story.

57
YOUR COMPETITORS' WEB STRATEGIES

Half of all Internet traffic starts with a search. Are you curious about what words and phrases (aka keywords) are generating traffic for your competitors? Do you wonder whether they're using Google Pay Per Click advertising and if so, for what keywords? How many web visitors are they getting? How much are they spending?

Amazingly, you can get answers to each of these questions for free! The tool is called www.SEMrush.com. "SEM" stands for search engine marketing, and what you'll discover is definitely a rush.

At SEMrush, enter each competitor's web address and click the "Overview" tab. The first thing you'll see is a traffic graph starting in 2010 showing paid and organic (free) monthly visitors.

Which of your competitors is winning, or losing? You'll likely discover that the ones growing consistently are also participating in social media. Blogging alone generates an average of 55% more web traffic.

Which tools are they using? Below the traffic graph you'll see a pie chart showing the percentage of their traffic that's coming from ads vs. organic terms. Are they generating meaningful business using Google's Pay Per Click (PPC) advertising? If so, are you?

Just a little farther down the page you'll see their top ten organic and paid keywords, their associated Google rankings, visitor counts, landing pages and equivalent or actual costs per click.

It's like breaking into their marketing department and stealing their strategic plan.

Half of all Internet traffic starts with a search. The data at SEMrush will help you get your fair share, and possibly a lot more.

58
PICTURE THIS

We are wired for stories. Everyone can remember something if they can picture it. If you need to share a lot of data, you need to wrap it in a story. Stories fit the mind in ways that data does not. Neuroscience and cultural anthropology affirm that a story is the best way to transfer information, to entertain, to sell, to accomplish your goals.

By telling compelling stories, we can actually plant ideas and thoughts, and trigger emotions in peoples' brains. It is only after we tell a story with a point that we create a CTA – call to action – for the audience.

59

CROWDSOURCING – THE WORLD IS FLAT

The next time you need to design something – say your new logo, your website or your product packaging – you can call your favorite graphics design firm. Or, you can "crowdsource" it instead and save a pile of money.

But saving money is not even the best part. When crowdsourcing, you'll likely see more than one hundred prospective designs before committing to the final design/designer. How cool is that?

You've heard that "the world is flat" (thank you Thomas Friedman) and this proves it! Social networking allows us to connect with people who have specific interests or specific skill sets.

At www.CrowdSpring.com you can reach roughly 200,000 "creatives" with graphics design skills, no matter where they live on the planet. Access the site and click on the appropriate project type to get started. There are roughly 50 categories. Use the handy red/yellow/green meter to determine the best "award" level for your type of project (it's not a job – it's a contest they can win).

And then be amazed as talented designers from around the world show you their best work before you must choose.

You don't take anything that is posted as a completed design. Instead, you rate the designs on a 1-to-5-star scale (5 being best) and give feedback.

The more direction you provide, the more iterations you'll get, and the better the designs will be. There's only one word for a service like CrowdSpring: unbelievable!

I've used this service a half-dozen times myself. The most I've ever spent was $1,201 for a complex e-commerce website design.

It's an amazing, almost magical process...unless you run a design firm.

60
KEYWORDS

Keyword all your stories so you don't sound canned. Never write out a script to memorize.

Take a sheet of paper, or create a document on your computer, and go through your presentation to find the most important words that trigger your stories.

For example, you might write *Paris* and that would be your keyword to trigger the travel story you want to tell.

Or you might write *Kate – ring,* to remind you of the story about your friend and the gift she gave you.

Be specific in your keywords. If you've been to Paris more than once, choose a keyword related to one specific trip, like a restaurant you'd been to.

Keep those keywords in front of you during your presentation, just in case you forget where you are.

That's all you'll need to jog your memory and keep going. Just like a pro!

61
BLOGGING

Companies that blog get 55% more Internet traffic. Seriously!

Here's why: Fully half of all Internet traffic starts with a search (mostly using Google). Since late 2011, Google has favored newer content over older. If you're blogging you're continuously creating new content so you're getting 55% more web traffic.

There are other benefits to blogging, too. You position yourself and your company as thought leaders, as experts. Blogging, when done in a personal way (be sure to include a photo of the content contributor), builds trust. Trust is the first step to a sale.

Blogging is a trust-building platform on a scale we've never seen before. So, what are you going to blog about?

Here's the key question: What would be valuable to your target audience? Think about it. If your content is not valuable to your target audience why would they devote their time and attention to it?

Obviously they won't, in which case you're the one wasting your time.

So what would be valuable to your target audience? This is a hard question to answer. Be brutally honest in assessing your strategy. If you can't find a compelling answer, I give you permission not to blog.

By the way, this same question applies to every form of social media including Facebook, Google+ and LinkedIn. Is your social media content valuable to them?

Let's assume you've developed a compelling value proposition, possibly based on educating your target audience about something they're interested in learning. How often should you post content?

Well, how often does your target audience really want to hear from you? If you post infrequently, you're missing an opportunity. If you post too often, your audience will become overwhelmed and will go away.

The other problem with posting too often is that's it's all but impossible to keep your content quality high. We're looking for the Goldilocks zone.

So, what's the right frequency for your audience?

If you sell to other businesses (B2B), the right answer might be once or twice a month. That would require just a few hours of writing each month.

Is that worth doing for 55% more Internet traffic?

62
WORDS, WORDS, WORDS

As Shakespeare said, "Words, words, words."

Use them! Use them descriptively and powerfully. Instead of saying, "My brother and I went to the park," create a picture of the person and the place that will put your audience in the movie.

"My brother Bill and I took a stroll through Oz Park, near my house. People always stare at Bill – he's almost 6'6" with red hair – and that day was no exception as we wandered around, looking at the statues of the characters in The Wizard of Oz. Did you know the author of the Oz book, Frank L. Baum, was a Chicago reporter?"

Use words to create context and contrast. Use words to move us emotionally, to create pictures in our minds, to put us in the reality of the situation, to experience it with you.

63
A BETTER WAY TO RUN A WEBSITE

Many people (as in 200,000,000) are familiar with blogging, one of the earliest forms of social media. But did you know that you can use a blog platform, WordPress, to run your entire website?

Check out my website, www.DialogConsulting.com as an example. On my website, you'll see a tab labeled "Blog" where I add posts once or twice a month. You'll also see a raft of other pages: "Home", "About", "Speaking", etc.

These pages are powered by WordPress. The big advantage of this approach to running your website is that you can change it quickly (and whenever you want), without knowing HTML, CSS, Java and the like.

Imagine, cost and cycle-time for making changes being virtually zero. If you can edit Microsoft Word, you can run a WordPress-based website. In fact, there's even a button on the WordPress toolbar called "Paste from Word." If you've got content in Word, you can publish it to your website with just a few clicks.

To get started, pick or create a WordPress theme. There are literally thousands of free WordPress themes and countless more for sale at modest prices (often around $30).

Or you can hire a designer to create a customized look for your website, as I did. Once you have your WordPress theme (and associated templates), you can log into your WordPress account, click "Pages" to access your set of pages and then select the one you want to edit (e.g., "Home", "About", etc.).

With WordPress, it's easy to add photos, videos and virtually any aspect of social media to your website. If you want to add a Twitter feed to your website, guess what? There's an app for that (actually called a "plug-in" in WordPress parlance).

There are plug-ins for virtually everything. For example, check out the calendar of events on my "Speaking" page. As a visitor, you can change the calendar view from "list", to "week", to "month", to "year". You can hover over a date and see where I'll be speaking. It's easy.

All this functionality comes from a free "Google Calendar" plug-in that is just as easy for me to use on the backend. In fact, I can add a calendar event to my website just by adding it to my iPhone calendar. How cool is that?

For search engine optimization (SEO) purposes, it's best to have your own instance of WordPress. In other words, don't run your blog at www.WordPress.org. Instead, GoDaddy, BlueHost, Rackspace and most other hosting providers feature a one-click WordPress install option for roughly $100 per year.

If WordPress doesn't provide exactly what you need, look for another open content management system (CMS) instead. Don't get locked into a proprietary CMS where you'll be trapped with your provider.

With WordPress (or Drupal, Joomla, etc.) you'll be able to switch providers whenever (if ever) required. And you can focus on managing content instead of managing geeks.

64
EVERY DAY IS A STORY

Many people say, "I have no stories."

Not true – we all do!

The day you were born is a story. Your first day of school is a story. Your first kiss. Getting your driver's license, the birth of your children...every day something happens, that's a story.

For some people, the challenge lies in uncovering their own stories. For others, it lies in figuring out the point of the story so that it's valuable to the listener. And for still others, it's trying to understand the CTA (call to action), also known as the takeaway.

With all the people I coach on all the different aspects of speaking, the most challenging aspect is figuring out those three components.

If you outline your speech with story-point-CTA as the body, you will never fail. The challenge is finding the universal message in your stories so you can use them to make your points.

65

IGOOGLE
DISCONTINUED...DO NOT PANIC!

On November 1, 2013 Google discontinued one of the most useful free tools on the planet. It was called iGoogle.

But, don't panic! I have a solution.

Even if you never tried iGoogle you know it was way cooler than the regular Google, because it had an "i."

iGoogle was an RSS dashboard (for the record, one of hundreds of "really simple syndication" tools). Ignore the lingo and techno-speak — it's actually nothing more (or less) than an information dashboard for whatever's valuable to you.

From now on as you surf the web, keep an eye out for the ubiquitous orange RSS icon.

You'll find it on blogs, podcasts, YouTube videos and everything else that's serialized (including media sites such as www.nytimes.com).

Using RSS is much like subscribing to a magazine, but in this case, it's for web content that's mostly free. Like a magazine, whenever the next issue is available (i.e., the next blog post, the next podcast, the next video episode), it comes to you automatically. RSS posts it directly to your dashboard, just like an old reliable mail carrier delivering your magazines.

Once you start looking for the orange RSS button, you'll see it everywhere. If the content on a given site is valuable to you, click the button and answer "yes" when asked whether you want to add it to your iGoogle desktop.

"But wait," you say, "iGoogle is gone."

Free market to the rescue!

When Google announced their planned shutdown of iGoogle (in a failed effort to get us to use Google+ instead), an enterprising team of coders created a replacement called www.igHome.com (as in the new home for everybody who used to use iGoogle). It even has a search box for Google right up top.

If you set igHome as your default browser homepage, you'll already be in the habit of looking at it regularly because you do Google searches many times a day. Just tell igHome to "remember me" (when logging in) and every time you go to search, you'll see your subscribed content neatly organized in its dashboard format.

Unlike email igHome content won't overwhelm you. Instead it will display just the three (or five, your choice) newest pieces of content from each of your sources. Don't feel compelled to read everything. Instead, scan the headlines and click just those items of interest, letting go of the rest.

Next time you return to igHome (aka your default page for searching Google), your content will be renewed. igHome and, more broadly RSS, is very much like a press clipping service of old. But in this case, it monitors not just press releases but also websites, blogs, Facebook pages, Twitter feeds, review sites and even traditional media.

In a world of information overload, it's one of the keys to staying on top of everything.

66
WE ALL HAVE STORIES

Remember that facts alone do not inspire. It's your story that creates the appetite for facts and makes them digestible.

Some of my clients deal mostly in data as they are economists, bankers, engineers, etc., and yet they surprise themselves when they start using stories to share their data, and see how well it's received.

Get rid of your "head trash." Stop telling yourself that you don't have stories or that you're not a good storyteller or that your audience isn't interested – get rid of the rest of your excuses.

Remember, it's a craft, just like tennis or chess or swimming. Even if you have some natural storytelling skills, it takes learning and practice in skill development to become a really great storyteller.

67
QUICK RESPONSE CODES

Have you noticed these things called Quick Response codes (more commonly called QR codes)? They're everywhere.

I see them in my local newspaper, on the sides of buildings, in magazine ads, on T-shirts and on bottles of wine.

What are they for? In short, they bridge people from the real world to your on-line presence. If social media is a conversation, what better way to engage your audience?

Scan to access a free
QR code generator

Last week, a woman handed me her business card and on it was a QR code. The QR code linked to a customer testimonial. Now that's how you take a prospect to the next level. Brilliant!

Here's how it works: Grab your smartphone and go to the App Store to download a "QR Reader" (there are countless providers). Then when you see a QR code, launch the app and point your phone at the code. No need to snap a photo or click a button.

The reader is continuously scanning for recognizable codes. As soon as it sees one, it jumps to the corresponding URL (aka web address).

So now that you've got the person online with your own QR code, what do you do with them? I recommend delivering an interesting, relevant or valuable mobile web experience – one optimized for small screens.

Please do not bring them to your homepage. That's boring and likely irrelevant.

Some people say QR codes are dead. I concede that they're no longer cool or cutting edge, but most people have QR Readers installed on their phones. If you have a valuable application for your target audience, I say try using them. The cost is essentially zero, so what are you risking?

To create a QR code, go to www.qrstuff.com or any other QR generator site. Enter your URL in the box and then download the resulting QR code. You can put QR codes on business cards, tradeshow booths, product brochures, etc.

When you use these codes, be sure to tell people why they should scan it.

The possibilities are endless.

68
EMOTIONAL TRANSPORTATION

Match your facial expressions to the various emotions you're describing. Use your hands the way you normally do – don't choreograph them; be as natural as possible.

Men, no hands in pockets. Ever! Take your keys and coins out of your pockets—no jingling!

Ladies, no girlie poses like sinking into one hip.

Every time you give a speech, you're in the "emotional transportation business." Take your audience on a journey.

This is the most important concept to grasp. Whether you're delivering a sales presentation or a state-of-the-industry address, your most important goal is to move your audience on an emotional level to want to buy your product or to accept your information. If you just give them facts, they can and will argue with you in their head.

Facts tell, stories sell. People buy on emotion and rationalize on logic.

Take us there!

69
HANDY LINK SHORTENERS

Recently, a friend sent me a link to a video he thought would be of interest:

http://play.simpletruths.com/movie/10-rules-for-success-v/?cm_mmc=ExactTarget-_-FR-_-11.02.12-_-GOLSmovie&j=23707&e=JohnQPublic@gmail.com&l=3516_HTML&u=1034392&mid=7001668&jb=20

Since this was in an email message, it was easy enough to click. Beyond being big and ugly, there's a simpler and more powerful way to share links. This is especially useful when you're sharing verbally, or when you require more concise communication.

Twitter anyone? This link alone (without any accompanying message) is 177 characters, well beyond Twitter's strict 140-character limit (at least as of the time I'm writing).

Interestingly, much of the information in the URL is tracking data that is not required to reach the destination site. Notice that roughly one-third of the way into the address there's a question mark. After that, the information is optional. You don't need the embedded date, email address, click source, etc., to access the target content. The following link will get you there just as effectively:

http://play.simpletruths.com/movie/10-rules-for-success-v

Still that's a bit long for Twitter, or to communicate verbally, so we have link shorteners. These services are provided by

Facebook, Twitter, su.pr, tinyurl.com (a surprisingly long name in a short business) and many others. My favorite is bit.ly.

These services create short addresses that automatically redirect you to longer addresses. On the bit.ly website (also known as bitly.com in case an address ending in 'ly' freaks you out), I paste my long link where it says 'Paste a long URL here to shorten' and voila! up pops my new short link:

http://bit.ly/RGFv4P

Note that the letters are case sensitive but there are just 6 of them; nice and easy.

Wait, it gets better. You can customize these links with easy-to-remember names. For one purpose or another I do this almost every week. For example, as a public speaker, I frequently share the address of my social media presentation handout. Both options below lead to the same place, but which do you think is easier to communicate?

www.bit.ly/social-media-4-biz or

https://app.box.com/files/0/f/87130995

That's excellent but it gets even better because bit.ly tracks click count, so you'll know exactly how often your content is accessed. This is especially handy when sharing a link with a single individual – you'll know whether they've clicked or not.

Links can be encoded so they can be read automatically by a Quick Response (QR) Reader app on a smartphone. Shorter links encode more cleanly and are more reliably scanned.

So, next time you want to share a link and track the clicks, use one of these handy link shorteners and maybe also a QR Code.

70
YOUR VOICE AS AN INSTRUMENT

Use your voice as the instrument it is; loud, soft, fast, slow, neutral, and the ultimate power to capture an audience...silence.

There are many other shading elements to the voice as well, including inflections and other dynamics. If you just learn to master the basics listed above, those alone will help your presentation be more engaging.

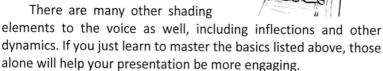

Vocal shading takes your audience on an emotional journey. Speak softly or slowly when telling a sad story, or when delivering bad news, data or statistics. Use a loud voice or fast speech to connote high energy or excitement.

And use the power of silence to let people think, feel and react.

71

GOOGLE +

Think about it: Why would you Google something if you could ask your friends or your professional associates? Isn't what they say likely to be more relevant and credible than some search engine's results?

If so, Facebook, LinkedIn and the other social networks are fundamental threats to Google's core business. Google cares deeply about social networking. Google has already "failed" at social networking three times, with Orkut, Wave and Buzz.

So Google+ represents Google's fourth try at social networking and even if they fail, I bet they'll try again. We could ignore any Google initiative at our peril given their immense market power. They control roughly three-quarters of the world's searches, including on the world's second largest search engine, YouTube.

Further, today more than half of all searches originate on mobile devices. You may have an iPhone but if so, you're in the minority. More than 80% of the world's smartphones run Google's Android operating system.

Yes, we could ignore any Google initiative at our peril.

On Facebook, almost everything you do is shared with your "friends" and with their "friends." The problem is that I use Facebook to share my family and personal pursuits. Typically I don't want this same information to be seen by my professional associates. It's not just me – we all have somewhat separate personal and professional personas and it's best if there's not too much cross-bleed.

If you think I'm crazy I ask you, "Do you dress the same for the office as you do at home on weekends?" In real life, we don't share everything with everybody. Instead, we have various circles of associates with whom we have different conversations.

Google+ is built on this foundation of "circles." When I connect with a person on Google+, I am required to place them in one or more circles. I can have a circle for "Family," a circle for "Friends," a circle for "Employees" and a circle for "Customers."

I can have a circle for anything.

With Google+ Circles, every time I post content I specify which circle or circles of people I want to allow to see it. Some things go just to my professional connections. Others go to friends and family. And yet others go exclusively to customers.

And when I view content on Google+, I don't have to look at everything from everybody. During the business day I can focus on the people in my employee and customer circles. In the evening and on weekends, I'll catch up with my family and friends via those circles.

Now, that's a better way to run a social network.

72
TAKING A RISK

Next time you create a speech, take a risk; try something unique for you, for your audience.

Depending on your tolerance for risk, there is no right or wrong. My challenge to you is to find your "discomfort zone" and enter it.

Do something that will surprise the audience, something unexpected. Find that risk factor that stretches you.

Perhaps it's just being vulnerable as you never have been. For some it might be using Prezi instead of PowerPoint. For others, it's simply switching from lecture mode to story mode.

Being a "safe" speaker is as boring for an audience as it is for you.

Use poetry or props, try a new interactive game...anything that challenges you will ultimately create joy for an audience.

73
PINTEREST: A SEARCH ENGINE FOR INTENTIONS

Have you heard of Pinterest? The last time I checked, Alexa.com (a handy Amazon service that measures traffic and demographics on all websites), Pinterest ranked as the 15th most popular website in the US and 35th worldwide.

Who are these people using Pinterest?

This is where things get interesting if your business serves a female demographic. According to Alexa, Pinterest users are heavily female, disproportionately in the coveted 25 – 34 age demographic, across all education levels, almost equally at work and at home.

This audience is incredibly important to car dealers, realtors, home builders, dentists, jewelers, gift shops, health clubs, etc. It might be easier to list the types of businesses that don't value this female demographic.

So, what is Pinterest? Think of it as an online scrapbook or corkboard to which you can pin things of interest to you: recipes, fashions, decorating ideas, crafts, photography, stuff related to your kids...just about anything else that's visual.

As the company self-describes: "Pinterest lets you organize and share all the beautiful things you find on the web. People use pinboards to plan their weddings, decorate their homes and organize their favorite recipes. Best of all, you can browse pinboards created by other people. Browsing pinboards is a fun way to discover new things and get inspiration from people who share your interests."

All that's good, but you know what Pinterest really is? If Twitter is about what you just did and Google is about what you want to do now, Pinterest is about what you're going to do in the future. It's a statement of intentions, of aspirations: what I'm going to cook tonight, what I'm going to wear tomorrow, what car I'm going to drive next week, where I'm planning to travel next month.

If you sell anything for women, get to know Pinterest. The stories of even small retailers finding monster audiences are legendary. No doubt men will eventually discover Pinterest as well. You might have to search a bit but (not to be too stereotypical) you can already find pins for guns, sports, geek technology, cars and fitness.

The applications are endless, even including people we'd like to arrest in the future. Seriously, the Mercury News based in Pottstown, PA has posted almost 100 photos of folks wanted by their local police (hey, if it's visual and interesting, it probably works on Pinterest). These people are purported to have committed crimes ranging from fraud to theft to assault.

Authorities receive almost daily tips resulting in a better than 50% increase in warrants served. The police are thrilled that the public is getting involved in improving their community.

So how can Pinterest work for your business?

Start by signing up and discovering what's interesting to you in your not too distant future.

74
INNER LADY GAGA

Bring out your inner Lady Gaga or your inner Herb Kelleher (former CEO of Southwest Airlines). Read and be inspired by his outrageous book, *NUTS*, as I was.

Don't hide behind PowerPoint or your industry as an excuse to be boring. Some of the sexiest topics in the world come out of the most conservative industries.

This isn't just about expanding your risk tolerance, this is more about shocking yourself and your audience with the unexpected, the outrageous.

Remember my mantra: *Be outrageous, it's the only place that isn't crowded™*.

75
CUSTOMER INTIMACY AND BUSINESS SUCCESS VIA PODCASTING

Few business leaders would argue with the dictum that the better you know your customers, the better you can serve them, and the more successful your business is likely to be.

When I was running TalkShoe, a "live podcasting" company I founded in 2005, every other week I did a "talkcast" inviting anyone who used our service to connect with me live or after the fact by listening to a recording.

Can you imagine talking to your customers 26 times a year? (If you'd like to listen to any of these talkcasts as models, almost one hundred of the recordings remain available at: http://www.talkshoe.com/tc/1517)

According to Wikipedia, "a podcast is a type of digital media consisting of an episodic series of typically audio or video files subscribed to and automatically downloaded through web syndication or streamed online to a computer or mobile device.

The word is a neologism derived from 'broadcast' and 'pod' from the success of the iPod, as audio podcasts are often listened to on portable media players." For my purposes, I'm talking about audio podcasts. In plain English, a podcast is an audio recording made to be listened to on an iPod (or iPhone, Android, etc.).

When thinking about audio content, consider this unique benefit: Busy people can listen to audio content while doing other things; driving, exercising, mowing the lawn, etc. You can't say that about video or text content. And everyone is busy these days!

There are countless ways to create a podcast. However, with TalkShoe you can record a podcast while involving live participants from anywhere on the planet, and streaming the resulting audio on the Internet.

As such, TalkShoe is a "live podcast" with participants calling in via phone or voice-over-IP (VoIP) from their computers. Think of it as a conference call on steroids. And TalkShoe is a free service.

With TalkShoe, hundreds of people can call into your live podcast (or talkcast as we call them). Literally thousands more can listen to the live audio stream online. To avoid chaos, everything is under "host" control, just like on a radio talk show.

The host can:

- Control whether the talkcast is public or private (by invitation only)
- Start and end recording
- Mute and unmute callers (callers use a "raise hand" signal to indicate the desire to talk)
- Text chat with callers
- Block caller text chat (on a per person basis)

And more...

Yes, people can listen to these live talkcasts after the fact because they're recorded. Better yet, if someone subscribes to your talkcast, every new recording is delivered to him or her automatically, just like subscribing to a magazine.

There are thousands of possible applications of talkcasting. On the TalkShoe website, you'll find 26 different content categories, most with over 1,000 separate sub-topics equating to more than one-million recordings to date.

Perhaps it's time to create a podcast series for your audience.

76

C.R.E.A.T.E.

Create new, unique,
compelling presentations

Risk, by trying something new
each time you present

Educate yourself on your topic
and never stop researching

Attitude towards your audience is positive

Time in honoring your allotted time

Enthusiasm for your topic and for the opportunity to share it

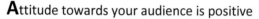

How long should a story be? The answer is, there is no right answer. It depends.

For my Keynote Kamp (one-on-one coaching with the purpose of designing an entire speech for a client), I worked with an exec who told me he wanted to stop being boring. His theme was leadership; his fear was not having a script, or memorizing his speech.

After much frustration and exploration, we wound up using the experience he'd had at the Boston Marathon bombing as the analogy and metaphor for various aspects of leadership. It was one story used throughout his entire speech and it was powerful and impactful, and he didn't have to memorize it because he had lived it.

Another speaker, in a sales speech, delivered a one-hour presentation on a story of the Teenage Mutant Ninja Turtles.

Think of incidences in your life, or things you've read or seen or heard about that have meaning to you, and they will have meaning for others when you create a story around them.

To begin, just start collecting them. And don't judge them.

77

LASTPASS

Almost everybody has the same problem. We have too many passwords to remember, which reminds me about one of my favorite apps on the planet: LastPass.

Before I describe LastPass, here's what you need to know about passwords: 80% of the world's so-called hacking is due to bad passwords!

You should use long, complicated passwords and you should never use the same password twice. The most common password is '123456.' If your password is '123457' you're not a genius; others have thought of that one too. Keeping passwords in a Word or Excel file named "My Passwords" might not be a best practice either.

But if you make every password 16+ characters long, always use letters, numbers, and special characters, and make every password unique, how will you remember all of them?

You don't have to remember. LastPass will do it for you.

LastPass is the last password you'll ever have to remember as it remembers all of your other passwords for you. So, you'll want to make your LastPass password extra-long, complex and unique, and protect it with 2-factor authentication, using either a text code to your phone or a fingerprint match or both.

Did I mention that LastPass works on PCs, Macs, Androids, iPhones and even Blackberries (if you still remember what those are/were)?

It's not like telling your browser to remember a password. That's only on that machine. With LastPass, a password saved on one device is available on all devices, even a brand new device you purchase tomorrow.

But it's more than that. LastPass generates passwords, auto-fills username and password fields on most websites, and even automatically changes passwords on many popular sites including LinkedIn. I mention this because in May 2016 LinkedIn announced they'd lost 100 million users' passwords to hackers.

LastPass also allows you to share access to websites with your spouse, your coworkers or anybody. Think: Bank accounts, family health insurance, company social media accounts and more.

What protects LastPass? Actually, two things: Military grade encryption before anything leaves your devices and the fact that they don't have or know your master password, so they can't lose it to the hackers. That's about as good as it gets.

So LastPass is the best encrypted vault for storing other sensitive stuff too, including social security numbers, credit card numbers and bank account numbers. And once you've done this, LastPass can autofill these fields too, along with addresses, expiration dates, CID codes, etc.

One key tip: If LastPass doesn't know your LastPass password, they can't give it back to you if you lose it. So don't forget this password!

The basic version of LastPass is free. The premium version is $1.00 per month, well worth it for an app this awesome.

78
VARIETY IS THE SPICE OF A PRESENTATION

Vary your speech with these:

- Anecdote: A short and amusing or interesting story about a real incident or person.

- Story: An account of imaginary or real people and events told for entertainment.

- Vignette: A brief evocative description, account or episode.

79
SNAPCHAT – WARN THE KIDS

There's a popular service that the younger crowd is using, now that they've spurned Facebook. It's called Snapchat.

Facebook reportedly tried to buy Snapchat for something like $3 billion. No deal.

By the way, in case you're not up-to-date on Facebook, you'll be interested to know that it's known as "a tool for connecting with old people."

Why use Snapchat instead? It's seems that the younger generation (call them Gen Z, born post-Y2K) is finally becoming aware of the downside of over-sharing, at least when done publicly where a parent, teacher or future employer might see it.

Snapchat allows you to send a photo or short video to a friend but with one important caveat: They can see it for just a few seconds before it goes poof (anywhere from 1 to 10 seconds as specified by the sender). It's supposedly deleted even from Snapchat's servers (no word about the National Security Agency's servers).

It seems like a great idea, right? So why do I say to warn the kids?

I have an iPad and an iPhone. These Apple products (and Androids, too) have a handy little feature that I use every day. Maybe you do, too. Whenever I have something on the screen that I want to save, say an article from The Wall Street Journal, I press the Power button and the Home button (the round one on the front screen) simultaneously – for just a fraction of a second – and voilà! it takes a picture of the screen. The article is saved forever in my photo roll. This very handy function is called screen snap or screen shot. If you've never tried it, I bet you'll find a reason to use it every day.

The problem is that you can even do a screen snap while viewing a Snapchat. Yes, it requires a little more dexterity because you have to touch and hold the screen to view Snapchat and then click the other two buttons simultaneously, but it's not that hard.

Snapchat even knows this can happen (and apparently can't prevent it). The app notifies a sender when an image has been captured but there's nothing the sender can do about it.

Bottom line: Snapchat is a very cool tool but it provides a false sense of security when sharing photos and videos. The pictures aren't always ephemeral. As with every other form of electronic communication, once you put it online you should assume it exists forever.

Like I said, warn the kids.

80
WAVING WILDLY...NOT!

I never choreograph my clients' hand gestures. Whatever you do, do it naturally onstage. There are many poses and gestures that DON'T work and I'm sure you can picture these: The military, the prayer position, the fig leaf...

Be as natural with your hands as you are with your voice, your body and your stories. If your audience is very large you might want to exaggerate them a bit so they're proportionate to the room, but don't be overly theatrical.

For example, a natural hand gesture when talking about an airplane or the sky would be to gesture towards it. Or when describing a person's height you can use a similar move. Focus on gestures that emphasize (not distract from) your main points. Use motions that are purposeful yet authentic. Use movements for emphasis or prompting or to describe.

No fiddling or nervous ticks – that will only serve to distract the audience from your message.

81
SOCIAL MEDIA: QUANTITY OR QUALITY?

In 2011 I discovered a social media measurement service called www.Klout.com (now part of Lithium Technologies). That's as in: "Who's got clout?"

My question is, do you have clout? Do you need it? How do you get it?

Greatly simplified, Klout.com measures a person's influence based on how many friends they have on Facebook and how many followers they have on Twitter.

I'm not saying that those are bad measures of influence. In fact, in business I want to influence the influencers so Klout.com may be a very valuable tool.

Still, as a social media professional I've made two radical decisions regarding business social networking.

#1: I don't try to be everywhere or to be all things to all people. All businesses have limited resources. Do one thing well rather than two things poorly. For business social networking I use only LinkedIn. Not Facebook, not Plaxo, not Ryze, not anything else.

#2: I connect with (or follow) only people I actually know. And respect. As a result, even though I was one of the first 100,000 members of LinkedIn, and roughly half a billion members have followed, today I have fewer than eight hundred connections.

But they're real connections. When I ask them for something, I usually get it. And when they ask me for something, I'm happy to assist.

Social networking is a lot like real life: When you invest in your relationships, those relationships pay dividends.

Yes, it's a little counterintuitive, but I say go for quality over quantity.

82

SO...

So, if I use the word 'so' at the beginning of every sentence what does it tell you about me or what I'm about to tell you?

Absolutely nothing.

'So' is the new 'you know' or 'um' – they are overused connectors – ways for us to fill a space that might feel awkward. We aren't even conscious of using them.

Practice your speech aloud to yourself, paying attention to those useless words, and then take them out.

Replace them with a pause at the end of your sentences. Get used to that. It may feel strange at first but you'll see, silence can be very powerful, and attention grabbing.

83
ENGAGE, THEN CONVERT

If somebody visits your homepage or follows you on social media, what value is that? Not very much.

When you consider your website and your social media initiatives, remember this mantra: Engage then convert. Engage then convert. Engage then convert. Ommmmm...

To engage your target audience, provide high-quality content that is genuinely useful to them. There are countless strategies to provide value.

One broadly applicable approach is to provide educational content, delivered regularly via a blog. Remember, people are busy and too much information will overwhelm them causing them to disengage. Put yourself into the mind of your target audience and ask yourself how often they really want to hear from you.

Aim for the Goldilocks zone – not too much content, but not too little either. 1-2 short blog posts per month may well be sufficient. And by short, I mean 300-500 words, like this chapter, that can be read in just a few minutes.

Such posts will require roughly 60-minutes to write and post (i.e., just 1-2 hours per month of your time to keep your audience engaged).

Make sure your content is genuinely valuable to your audience. As one of my favorite bloggers once said: "Content isn't king. Usefulness is king."

Think seriously about your target audience and your potential engagement strategies.

Engage, then convert.

To convert, start by deciding what you want your web (or social media) visitors to do and then create associated calls-to-action to accomplish that. An example of a call-to-action would be, "Have a salesperson contact me."

But it's rare that a prospect will go straight to the close, so create a series of conversion steps. An easy initial conversion might be, "Subscribe to our newsletter."

To increase the conversion rate of that call-to-action, give to get: "Sign up for my newsletter and get my list of 10 things NOT to do in social media."

Consider the subsequent conversion steps and associated calls-to-action that are important to you and place these appropriately throughout your website and your social media initiatives.

Lead your visitors to your desired destination.

Engage, then convert.

84
UNDERSTANDING YOUR PURPOSE

Understanding your purpose in storytelling will help you choose the right stories to accomplish your goal. Decide if your story is to inspire or to educate. Are you using a story to simplify complex data or do you want to launch a new movement?

Are you telling stories to entertain or to honor?

Is storytelling your vehicle for causing people to embrace change?

Stories have power. Every speech, every story should have a purpose that is real and visible to an audience or else they won't care and will tune out.

And remember, that purpose needs to tie into what *they* want, what *they're* expecting.

It's all about them.

85
WEBSITE OR APP

I've offered a lot of advice about your company's website: Building it on a content management system (CMS), using the principles of responsive design, providing compelling content, using calls to action (CTAs) to drive "conversions," and measuring everything. But there's another important consideration resulting from the explosion in smartphone ownership.

Remember, smartphones and other mobile devices outsell traditional computers (desktops and laptops) by an 11-to-1 ratio. In the near future, that ratio will likely approach 20-to-1. The problem with these mobile devices goes beyond just their small screens. The question to think about is this: "What does a person using a mobile device want or need?" The answer is likely quite different than if they're visiting your website using a desktop machine or notebook computer.

Perhaps it's time to design your website for mobile devices and then adapt your website for traditional computers, instead of vice versa. This philosophy is called "mobile first."

Mobile first is not just about screen size. Put yourself into the mind of your mobile visitor. If they're on your website using their smartphone, isn't it more likely (than if using a desktop) that they're interested in driving directions? How about videos? Those are fantastic on a small screen. What about finding your phone number?

What else might they value given that they're probably not in their office? Which calls to action might be more relevant in such situations? Mobile first thinking opens up countless new questions.

But hold the phone (pun intended)!. What percentage of the time does a typical smartphone user spend navigating in a browser vs. using other apps on the phone? The disappointing answer (at least for webmasters everywhere) is 10% and dropping. So, 90% of the time there's literally zero probability that a smartphone user is visiting your website.

If we're really thinking "mobile first," perhaps we'll conclude that our next investment shouldn't be in buffing up our website but rather in building an app for our target audience instead. Radical thinking, I know.

Just this week, I visited a website called Duolingo.com on my iPhone (side note: Duolingo was recently Apple's *App of the Year)*. The Duolingo website was a simple and beautiful mobile first design that had a small banner at the very top: Click here to install the Duolingo app instead.

Now that's the best of both worlds.

86
FACTS TELL, STORIES SELL!

If you can't tell it, you can't sell it. Customers buy from people they like. Telling stories enhances your likeability factor so that it all comes full circle and you win the sale.

Whether you call it a case study or a story or anything else, the bottom line is that there's a narrative and it's that narrative that delivers the power of your message, the point of your speech, your reason to deliver.

I often tell my clients to get comfortable with being uncomfortable. Stories are your vehicle for making information come alive.

Facts alone will not do that.

87

CONVERSION STEPS

I see many business people who engage in social media programs simply because others do. Further, they make no attempt to quantify the value of such initiatives and therefore tend to under invest. In turn, social marketing brings few new customers to their company and in a self-fulfilling prophecy, it's not worth investing more. There is no guaranteed inherent value in having a LinkedIn Company Page follower, a Facebook "Like," a Ning member or a Twitter follower.

Rather, its value depends on your ability to motivate the participant to voluntarily execute your desired actions. After all, you're in business to make money not to make friends, right? Consider the value of the following sequence of actions.

If:

1. a LinkedIn company page visitor or follower
2. clicks to your "Products and Services" tab, then
3. notices and reviews some of the eighty-three recommendations for that product, and
4. clicks on the description of your "Unified Data Center" service (to use a hypothetical product example), then
5. sees and clicks on the link to your blog post about that service, and
6. reads that post and, finally
7. clicks the button to "Have a Salesperson contact me," you've achieved the desired outcome for that person.

What I've described here are seven sequential "conversion" steps from being a random member of LinkedIn to being a self-qualified prospect for your company.

Similar conversion steps are definable for any social media participant whether reading your blog, following you on Twitter, participating in your external Ning network or Liking you on Facebook.

Have you considered the conversion objectives and associated steps for your social media and digital marketing programs (including website and landing page visitors)? Once understood and explicitly defined, your conversion steps can be tracked, measured and even valued.

Your marketing team or outside agency partner should be thrilled to tackle this task because they can then prove their value to your organization.

If you want to maximize your sales and marketing profits, then know your intended conversion steps and measure their effectiveness.

88
DRESS THE PART

Dress appropriately for your audience, the venue and the location. Don't wear a three-piece suit if you're talking to a group in the Bahamas.

When I spoke to a group of college frat boys on spring break in Cabo San Lucas, Mexico you can bet I didn't wear a navy blue suit and white blouse (not that I even *own* that!). I looked professional but accessible.

The general rule is to be one step above your audience. Avoid wearing anything that might come between you and them.

Dress to fit the audience and your brand.

89
KEEPING UP IN A WORLD OF ACCELERATING CHANGE

People ask me all the time, "Dave, how do you keep up with all this social media and mobile technology? It's evolving so rapidly!"

There's a good reason for this question but it applies more broadly to virtually any industry and to life in general.

We're reportedly dealing with roughly ten times the amount of information we faced just three years ago. And we'll be dealing with roughly ten times more information three years from now. And ten times more three years after that.

First, don't try to learn alone. Instead, find the blogs, the technical forums, the LinkedIn groups and the other trusted sources where you can learn from myriad appropriately-focused individuals.

That's why you're reading this book, right?

Second, find time for continued learning. You're too busy you say? Au contraire, I say, if you just change the media mode.

All of us actually have lots of time for learning, when our bodies are occupied but our minds are not.

I'm talking about when we're driving, exercising, mowing the lawn. During these kinds of activities we can learn by listening to audio content on our smartphones.

Audible.com (part of Amazon.com) has an app and 200,000 audio books available for $14.95 apiece. I recommend "The Four Hour Work Week," "The Tyranny of E-mail," "Team of Rivals," "Steve Jobs," "The Innovators," "Brain Rules," and the always classic "Think and Grow Rich," to name just a few of the audiobooks I've listened to in the past few years.

I never would have found time to actually read these.

The other form of audio content I recommend is podcasts, another app, and content produced for listening on your smartphone (whether iOS, Android, or Windows).

I recommend "Dan Carlin's Hardcore History," (no, it's not about the porn industry), "NPR Science Friday," "The Memory Palace," "99% Invisible," and "Planet Money," among literally countless others.

Yes, we're all crazy-busy.

But we still have time to listen and learn.

90
WHEN IN DOUBT, LEAVE IT OUT

Be careful of inappropriate language, sarcasm or offensive gestures. With today's multi-generational, multi-cultural audiences, it pays to do some research about the meaning of certain words and gestures so as not to offend.

If you speak internationally you must be extra diligent about words in translation, gestures or statements that mean something else in another language or culture.

91

MEASURE IT!

What are the five most important words in a businessperson's vocabulary? Perhaps you answered, "The customer is always right."

I love my customers but I have another answer: "What gets measured gets done."

It's an incredibly powerful concept in business and in life. Show people the metrics, help them understand how to impact them and watch the magic happen.

It's an idea so powerful that when then Veterans' Affairs Secretary Eric Shinseki attempted to eliminate a massive scheduling backlog by setting an objective that all new patients be seen by a doctor within 14 days – apparently without adding more doctors – well, you know the rest of the story. Faced with an important measurement that was impossible to meet, staff members invented a sophisticated way to game the system (aka cheat).

Setting reasonable goals is a topic for another chapter. Here, I want to talk about the power of measuring important things like your web traffic and your social media engagement. Remember that Google Analytics is your tool for measuring these things.

I think that Google Analytics is even better than the tools I had to pay for back in the day (ClickTracks and Webtrends, to name two), and it's free.

If you've new to this, start with one key measurement. I recommend tracking "engaged" web sessions, meaning those visitors staying longer than 0 - 10 seconds. The rationale for excluding the shortest duration group of visitors is that it's likely they departed quickly because they arrived at an unintended destination. Further, it's hard to believe that any visitor derived significant value (or moved closer to becoming a customer) based on an average 5-second, single-page visit.

If you can assign (aka guesstimate) the value of an engaged web visitor, this metric can be converted to dollar value via straight multiplication and can be useful in assessing the effectiveness of the digital team's overall efforts (and in calculating associated ROI).

What gets measured gets done.

92
IS HUMOR NECESSARY?

People often ask if you have to use humor as a professional speaker.

The answer is, only if you want to get paid.

No matter what the speech topic is, and particularly if it's a very serious one, you must use some humor. People need a break from too much info or too much data or too much gravity.

They simply need to laugh occasionally to release the tension, and to stay with you.

And remember, your humor doesn't have to cause raucous laughter – a chuckle will do the job nicely.

Humor is the great connector. Make an audience laugh and they will love you. You don't have to tell jokes; you simply need to pay attention to what's funny to your particular audience.

And self-effacing humor endears you to an audience more than anything else.

93
MEASURE IT (PART 2)

Perhaps the most commonly tracked website metric is web hits. It turns out that "hits" is an acronym that stands for "How Idiots Track Success."

Instead, you want to track web visitors (aka web sessions) which eliminates the radical over-counting inherent in hits (one visitor can generate hundreds of hits).

After you get a handle on your total web visitors (see my previous chapter), begin to drill down (aka *segment* your traffic) so you can gain additional insight and control.

I recommend proceeding with:

- Direct visitors – those people who typed your web address directly into their browser address bar. Tracked over time, this metric will tell you how well your overall sales and marketing efforts are working.

- Organic search visitors – those folks who typed a word or phrase into Google or other search engine and then clicked on your result. Half of all Internet traffic starts with a search and more than three-quarters of clicks are on the organic (free) results.

- Paid search visitors – those surfers who clicked on one of your paid ads (think: Google AdWords). While this represents less than one-quarter of search traffic, if you make more money from paid search visitors than it costs you to attract them, keep it going. This can be especially effective for picking off prospects searching for your competitors' names.

- Referral visitors – those people who came from your Facebook page, your LinkedIn page, your Twitter page or any other external website. Think about it: A "Follower" or a "Like" has no inherent value if you're not converting at least some of them into customers.

After you start tracking these metrics, you'll want to track the next 10, and the next 10…

If you're not yet measuring the effectiveness of your sales, marketing and social media initiatives, one of two potential tragedies is afflicting you. Either you're spending money in the wrong places and not getting a sufficient return on your investment, or you're getting a fabulous ROI but should be investing far more.

In reality, it's probably a mix of both.

So how are your various social media initiatives and your website actually serving your company?

It's time to measure and find out.

94
BUT I'M NOT A COMEDIAN!

No one expects you to be Jerry Seinfeld. You can find humor in anything.

Create a humor journal. Every day there's something that makes you laugh. Write it down or set up a file folder on your computer or phone, and make note of it there.

How do you find the humor? Just pay attention in your daily life – it's everywhere! And then collect it, but don't judge it. It's the judging or the "head trash" that makes us think it's not good enough.

You'll see...when you have to make that speech or roast or toast, or whatever, you'll read through your humor journal and crack yourself up. You'll have years and years of things you personally find funny, things you're comfortable with, to use at your discretion.

You'll find humor in what your kids say, what's on a bumper sticker, on a t-shirt, in a TV interview, in the newspaper.

Just don't buy books on humor; they're mostly old and stale and overused.

Find original humor in your life.

95
IT'S A B2I WORLD

Recently, I was speaking to a group of CEOs in California about using social media for business. The host introduced me to the somewhat skeptical, mostly Baby Boomer generation audience by suggesting that whether their companies sell B2C (business-to-consumer), B2B (business-to-business) or B2G (business-to-government), they all sell B2I (business-to-individual).

It's a brilliant observation and an acronym that I intend to use regularly from now on.

Recall the old sales adage that "people buy from people." It's especially true for B2B companies.

What "social" allows us to do (on LinkedIn, by writing a blog, by using Google+ Circles, etc.) is turn our organizations back into the people who are the company.

In fact, maybe it's not so much B2I as it is I2I (individual-to-individual) just like the good ol' days (when it actually was eye-to-eye).

Social allows us to connect with far more prospects than we ever could meet face-to-face. These new tools are more efficient and more effective for today's communication and collaboration challenges. Remember when you first had to learn to use a fax machine, a pager, an email account or a Blackberry? Tools evolve.

Social media and social networking are just the newest part of the communication continuum. If you've not yet taken advantage of these new tools, start by reframing your thinking.

Social media and social networking are powerful new tools for your B2I business, for more effective communication with employees, prospects, customers and partners.

96
THE 5 Ws

You always want to know the 5 Ws:

Who are you speaking to by demographics and psychographics?

What are you speaking about?

When will you be speaking?

Where will the event be held?

Why are you speaking on the topic, based on client goals and objectives?

97
WHEN SOCIAL MEDIA FAILS

There are myriad reasons that business social media initiatives fail. Here are some potential problems and possible solutions:

1. They're ignoring you because you're pushing marketing information at them (aka monologue), instead of connecting in a dialogue as a real person. Ask yourself, WWMD (what would Mikki do)? Include an interesting picture of yourself and display some personality!

2. Your customers aren't interested right now because they don't require a continuing relationship with your business. If you sell real estate, your prospects will engage only when they need to buy a property (rarely).

3. In this case, use search.twitter.com to find people in your area tweeting about house hunting and the like. There are more than half-a-billion tweets per day. Listening on Twitter is like having ESP; you'll know exactly when they're looking for what you do. Reach out to them at exactly that moment.

4. They're not engaging because you're using the wrong platform. Facebook is great for B2C (business-to-consumer). It's often worthless for B2B (business-to-business). If you sell to other businesses, consider using LinkedIn (to network

or to share valuable information), Ning (to create a knowledge base/community) or WordPress (to write a blog). Use the same platform your audience does.

5. They're not paying attention because you're adding to the noise and information overload. Instead, figure out how to provide something of value to your customers. If you run a chauffeur service, have your drivers tweet about traffic conditions or airport delays (but not when they're actually driving, please). People will follow them to get valuable on-the-ground updates and your company will always be top of mind.

6. Customers don't know about your social media initiatives. Your content may be superb but if they don't see it, well...

7. You need an awareness plan. Highlight your initiatives on your business card, in your email signature, on your homepage, in your email marketing and on your front door.

8. They're engaging and you're not responding. It sounds absurd but I've seen countless examples of a customer asking a question or posting a complaint, only to be ignored. Social media is a dialogue and you have to hold up your end of the conversation. This is not a set-it-and-forget-it activity.

If your audience is not engaging with your social media, figure out if it's one of these problems and address it accordingly.

Otherwise, you're just wasting your time.

98
THEY WON'T LAUGH IF THEY'RE UNCOMFORTABLE

Be aware of the difference between self-effacing humor and dwelling on personal negatives. Don't apologize for your weight, your accent or anything else in a way that makes an audience uncomfortable.

Do use self-effacing humor, as that lets your audience know you don't take yourself too seriously.

That's an endearing quality and your audience will connect to that.

99
THE POWER AND BENEFITS OF SOCIAL MEDIA

From my vantage point "social" has the power to transform your business for the better. Here are just a few of the benefits you can realize:

- Social networking allows you to expand your knowledge exponentially.

- Social media tools accelerate learning by inviting input from a wide range of stakeholders, including current and potential customers, dissatisfied customers, team members and industry experts, all of whom are willing to freely give you their ideas and share their expertise.

- The tools allow you to create forums in which people can build on each other's ideas, creating synergies and developing solutions well beyond the capacity of individuals

- Social networking provides bi-directional learning, giving you a tremendous return on your efforts.

- Social media invites current and potential customers to tell you how to improve products and services. At the same time these people are giving you priceless information they're learning about your company and what you have to offer.

- Social networking helps you fill your pipeline. People who engage with you in social media are not necessarily ready to buy. However, your continuing conversation keeps you top of mind. When people in your network are ready to buy they will already know you, trust you and be informed about your offerings. Assuming you are providing value to your target audience (a fundamental rule for social media), your audience and your pipeline will continue to grow.

- Social media helps you outrun your competition.

- Social media tools give you access to industry experts and competitors' former employees who are willing to share information. The tools allow you to quickly get up to speed on any industry by reviewing specialized discussion threads.

- Social media tools also allow you to contact prospects immediately after they express dissatisfaction with your competitors, and they allow you to create situations in which new opportunities come to you.

- Social networking has the power to increase internal knowledge and efficiency.

- Social media tools allow you to collect corporate knowledge in a central location, eliminating the constant need to email and search email. The savings in time and reduced frustration make a substantial difference in efficiency. What's more, these tools allow you to capture and easily access knowledge that typically is lost when an employee leaves your company. They allow current employees to build on each other's ideas.

If these benefits sound compelling to you, it's time for your company to get social.

100
THE ART AND HEART OF STORYTELLING

Parker Palmer, who hails from my hometown of Chicago and is a well-known author, educator and activist has been quoted as saying, "Human connection comes about through story, it is our shared story that allows us to connect, to empathize and relate."

Real learning happens heart to heart, not head to head.

Storytelling is a timeless tradition. We're wired for communicating through, and learning from, stories.

Stories are not meant to tell us how to think, stories are meant to give us something to think about.

As I cross the country speaking and coaching executives who must share data in their presentations, I find a big disconnect.

Storytelling has become a lost art in business. PowerPoint has crushed our natural instincts to tell stories. We've become so bogged down in corporate speak, jargon and facts, that we've lost what is most natural to us all.

Another challenge is that people know how to talk, so they think they know how to speak. Speaking without learning the craft is like making wine without grapes. Using stories helps you persuade, influence and inspire. Stories fit the mind in ways that data does not.

The more data one uses the less connected we feel; the more human interest, the greater our sense of connection.

Instead of telling our valuable stories we think we feel safer sharing opinions, ideas and beliefs rather than our lives.

Try sitting down with your life and your business and sorting them out as stories. Just as social media has the power to transform your business, being a good speaker can transform your life and the lives around you, business and personal.

To be a change agent, to get your ideas across, to teach a lesson, you first must engage your audience – you must connect with them, whether it's an audience of one or one-thousand.

At work, everyone naturally gravitates toward using logic and statistics because it seems more professional, but the truth is that emotion always works better because that's the way to reach hearts and minds. Emotion allows people to see the real you, which is authenticity. Storytelling is about authenticity. It allows the real you to shine through.

That's when connection happens...to an audience, to a client, to a prospect, to a family member, to life itself.

It was my intention to share with you my tips on the craft of speaking and the power of storytelling to inspire you to give better presentations.

Communication in business is key, and being a powerful presenter is one of the top success skills you can master.

The mediocre speaker...tells

The good speaker...explains

The superior speaker...demonstrates

The great speaker...inspires